MW01714957

WALK IN THE LIGHT

Welcome

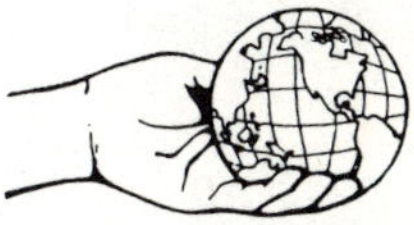

WALK IN THE LIGHT

Messages from the Ascended Masters

CHANNELED AND RECEIVED BY
Anna May Cottrell
and
Nancy H. Wikingstad

Blue Dolphin Publishing
1987

For information, address:
Blue Dolphin Publishing, Inc.
P.O. Box 1908, Nevada City, CA 95959

ISBN: 0-931892-12-0

Library of Congress Catalog Number: 87-15821

Library of Congress Cataloging-in-Publication Data

Walk in the light

1. Spiritual life. I. Cottrell, Anna May, 1929-
II. Wikingstad, Nancy H., 1908- . III. Title :
ascended masters.
BF1290.W28 299'.93 87-15821
ISBN 0-931892-12-0

Printed in the United States of America by
Blue Dolphin Press, Inc., Grass Valley, California

9 8 7 6 5 4 3 2 1

CONTENTS

THERE "I AM"

You seek me, ever wanting to know
Where I Am, how I came and how I go.
Then look deep within—then deep without;
For in the silence or in the noisy shout—
        There "I Am."

Listen to the laughter of a child,
See the tears thru which he smiled,
Behold the masterpiece from the artist's hand,
For in meek obedience and strong command—
        There "I Am."

In carefree youth and age'd brow
Past, present, future, the ever now
In all inanimate and animate things;
Perceive the source from which they spring—
        There "I Am."

In mountain streams, river or sea,
In grass, trees, flowers, birds or bees,
In antiquity, or mystery of the newly born,
Search the sunlight, the rainbow, the storm—
        There "I Am."

Some call me truth, some light, others love,
Wise as the serpent, but gentle as the dove
In surgeon's hand or in scholar's brain,
Of lonely hermitage or lover's twain—
        There "I Am."

All in all, beginning to end—
Sweetheart, parent, foe or friend
Far and near, high or low
Thru all time in all space, you'll know—
        There "I Am."

The restless, stirring soul within thee
Spurs you ever on to find true reality.
In that silence, the still small voice,
The unspoken word can be heard, rejoice!
        There "I Am."

Anna May Butcher - 1962

SOUGHT I AND BECAME

Wisdom's garments sought I to wear—
The Crown of Love to halo my hair.
The Scepter of Dominion for my hand,
On Threshold of Cosmic Light to stand.

Suddenly; a thousand blazing suns enfold—
The Flame of the Sacred fire I behold,
All in All, One with One, yet, I am I—
Spark energies with fire, then surges high.

Humbly the "Seamless Robe" I wear,
The Crown of Love diadems my hair.
Scepter of Dominion I hold high,
Eternal, Infinite, Immortal, Am I.

On the Threshold of Truth's transcendent light,
I perceive Creation with Soul Light.
I Am the Atom, the Atom Am I;
Elohim, Cyclopea, the all-seeing eye.

I am the music of the Spheres,
The hymn of Creation ringing clear.
The song is the song of Love.
All shall be below as it is above.

Anna May Butcher - 1962

FOREWORD

IN THE EARLY DAYS OF the sixties, a group of young women came together in my home in the Canal Zone in the country of Panama, and we all were interested in the higher wisdom that the Ascended Masters were channeling through Anna May Cottrell, nee Anna May Butcher. It was a great joy and enlightenment to our souls to partake of the wisdom of the Masters, and this is the purpose of this book—*Walk in the Light*. We wish to share it with you.

In those days the esoteric wisdom was not widely known, studied or contemplated upon as it is today, but we were ones that were reaching for the ultimate in spiritual understanding, and through our own spirits we were well aware of wisdom beyond that being brought forth in the Orthodox Churches of that time. Because of this non-acceptance of the Occult wisdom, we were admonished by the Masters "Dare to Be, Dare to Do, and Be Silent."

In these sessions with the Masters we were emersed within their light and vibration. We knew we were in the company of spiritual beings, and we felt and we knew we were walking with them in wisdom's way. I bring our experiences to you in "Walk In The Light" that you, our readers, may find joy in sharing the words and lessons that came through and that you may come to a realization that you as God's children play (or work) out your own part in the panorama of individual unfoldment. In all this we too came to the understanding that there would be a great unfoldment in Earth's destiny, and that Earth would make a great advancement into the Solar Confederation of Planets in the coming New Age—a new dispensation.

Never before in the history of this age have the Masters told of the part they play in the advancement of this planet as well as their concern for individual unfoldment. Today the Masters are announcing their part in this great drama that is taking place. Our Commander-in-Chief, Jesus, the Christ, is making himself known by voice contacts and is being seen clairvoyantly. As he comes through he is announcing himself as Sananda (San anda), which name I shall hereafter use. His spiritual Father gave this name to him at his birth on Earth.

There is much concern about the peaceful emergence of this planet we call earth into another planetary orbit, because the plain truth is that the majority of earth's inhabitants have not learned their ABC's and are not living the great lessons that Sananda brought 2,000 years ago, namely: love, compassion, and the peace that life should and could be lived in harmony with their fellow man.

The Light Workers of today who are aware of the Masters' teachings are listening to their words, are in accord with what is coming forth from the Masters and the Hierarchy about conditions within the races of men, and they are being urged to help redeem the incalcitrant individuals—especially those who cannot have compassion for those of different belief systems, as well as knowing that planet Earth is in need of help as well. Planet Earth is a reflection of the distress in man.

The great Ascended Master, St. Germain, a tireless worker, beginning with the forming of the Declaration of Independence for the colonies, has always guided and claimed America as his baby.

St. Germain and Sananda in all their channelings through the Light Workers are admonishing the workers to lay aside their personal growth to give time in meditation in daily sending and using the three-fold flame—Blue, representing the WILL, Emerald Green THE HEALING LIGHT, the Violet Flame to nullify and transmute the negativity present on all planes of existence, including the astral plane, giving as much time as they can spare from their daily activities. Our scientists have chosen to be oblivious of the damage that has been done to Earth because of indiscriminate use of the atomic power.

Because of this great need for the cooperation of all people, I am going to set forth a technique for using the three-fold flame.

You can start at any chosen point you so desire on the planet or in America, OR AT A POINT OF YOUR CONCERN AT THE TIME, and vision this three-fold flame in that place, and then bring your vision around in concentric circles—seeing the circles ever becoming larger and larger covering the point you have chosen. Your work in that instance is done.

In covering our National Capitol do it in this way and see the three-fold flame touching the judicial system, the Army, the Air Force, the Navy, the Coast Guard, the Marines and the Pentagon. (You can keep in mind while doing the capitols that there is already a strand of esoteric light built from capitol to capitol in the United States, and that you are only strengthening the links already created by another.) There is not a point in world governments and their capitals, even remembering there are civilizations in inner earth, that does not need the transmuting flame to overcome the negative actions and thoughts.

You can adopt the technique of visioning the blue, green and violet lights raining down as shimmering and scintillating petals of colors, creating in your mind the beauty of the important thing you are doing in *using the tools of the Infinite.*

As you use this activity be aware of the definite results you are accomplishing. You being with the Masters in this critical time is indeed a blessing to the overall need. With the energies sent from the Solar and Cosmic Sources focused through your minds in meditation and out to the planet, so will the earth be changed. You being with the concern of the Masters is of critical importance for the continuation of the evolution of man and the evolution of this planet. In this cycle can come the transformation of the eventual liberation from Astral Thraldom. We are nearing the battle between the forces of light and darkness which some will call Armageddon.

May all who read these words join forces in unity, understanding, love and blessing to our Earth and its inhabitants. We must reverse what man has done to himself as well as to other men in polluting the planet with atomic radiation. Earth indeed cries for help along with mankind. It is up to all who love their beautiful planet to put their hands to the plough and vision for a beautiful Earth as it was created in the beginning.

Let the words of Sananda carry you all to a Blessed Ascension into the light, and, as he would say: "My peace I give to you that you may share it effectively."

Nancy H. Wikingstad,
Collaborator

THE GREAT INVOCATION

From the point of Light within the Mind of God
Let Light stream forth into the minds of men
Let light descend on Earth

From the point of Love within the Heart of God
Let Love stream forth into the hearts of men
May Christ return to Earth

From the Center where the Will of God is known
Let Purpose guide the little wills of men
The purpose which the Masters know and serve

From the Center which we call the race of men
Let the plan of Love and Light work out
And may it seal the door where evil dwells

Let Light and Love and Power restore the plan on Earth

AS A TEACHER

HOW MANY THREADS are needful in the weaving? How many lives are represented by these threads? How many weavings are found in the threads of your lives? How many weavings to make the pattern whole? Behold! many are to come, many are to be united, and many to go forth. Behold! it as it was said unto you—the Mother Flame united with the Father Flame becomes one central fire and many torches will come to dip within the flame and be ignited and sent forth. Behold! to the farthest corners of the earth will this light go and these torches will burn. Behold! even as you served at the altar, do you now also serve. Yes, you begin to comprehend the truth that lies therein, and you shall soon behold it and the mind shall comprehend it as it is in spirit and as being expressed through the physical form of the bodily manifestation.

BEAM

AND WHY BEHOLDEST thou the mote that is in thy brother's eye, but considerest not the beam that is in thine own eye? St. Matthew 7, vs. 3.

I refer to our brother, as he spoke—"See not the beam in thy brethern's eye, least though removest the splinter from thine own, and, therefore, can see clearly to help thy brother to remove the beam from his own eye." Simple words of truth, yet man spends years studying and not comprehending; teaching, but not adhering to; advocating, but not becoming the example.

"Seeth thou the beam in thy brother's eye and remove the mote from thy own." Herein is a problem with many people who behold a work they feel of their own doing, a creativity of their being and behold not the Genius, the Creator. They behold only that which they have within themselves as the faults in others, and only by removing these things from within themselves will they see they were not in their brother. I am speaking from an objective point of view, not as a personal point, and I speak not as a personal point of those here, but those who are absent.

BECOMING A CHRIST

YOU BECOME STRENGTHENED within the inner structure. You have found within yourself, even at the point of desperation, a calmness, a reliability, a security, though it may be sensed more often than fully felt; nevertheless, this is and is becoming and growing stronger. In the passage of time it will be as an unseen ocean and become as an island where others may find refuge, strength and light, where others may find compassion and understanding. You have been told to be a "Christ" and to know a "Christ," and to understand a "Christ" is to become a "Christ," as he became.

Once your feet have been upon this path, the crown of thorns and the weight of the cross becomes heavy, for grief and pain are the greater teacher, and love bears the world, for in knowing the compassion and the understanding is the "Christ" suffered and born, is to have lifted the weight of not only one's self, but someone else's, and therefore, when one comes to you and cries out, "Help me, speak unto me, heal me," you can do all things without limitation in the freedom of the spirit.

BEGINNING

AVE! AVE! INITIUM! and I speak in the words of the beginning. In the beginning was light, and even as in the ending it will be light, but in the valley is found the darkness. I say unto them that travel the valley road, lift your eyes ever to the hills from whence cometh this strength, for one day you shall climb the mountain, travel the hilltop, and shall know only light. In seeking truth and being a servant to truth, seeking the light and being bearers of the light, in seeking divine love and giving it forth in its divinity are all things. How often have you been told "my kingdom is not of this world," and yet my reward is with me? The things of the earth were not promised as a reward. The reward is in Him who overcame the earth. Yes, in your overcoming are the rewards of spirit and not the things of the earth, for that which are of the earth are the unrealities; they pass away, and become as nothing, but the things of the spirit are the realities and pass not away, but are eternal. He who looks for a reward within your world will find it not and yet he who seeks to serve with a humble heart shall be exalted and shall be glorified for he seeks not the glorification of self, but to glorify the Father within him that sent him into being. Herein lies the rise and fall of great things, for in the rising was the sincere desire of service and the glorification of God, but in the fall when he took upon himself to glorify self and not God, let his own self, or ego, rule the temple body and the mind, and he in the ultimate lost all things.

BEING

YOU ARE BEING. You are gathering soul knowledge. Each life you have gathered beingness, but it is now time of your harvest that you must share that which you have gained and gathered. You understand! Then know that these things are necessary in life, but also inactivity. Many times during an inactive period, one may choose not to take up the activity, but then this is their choice, or one may resume a former activity and develop it fully. This also is their choice. One may be given a task or a mission to fulfill, yet the answer is still of that instrument. In no wise does it mean no progression, yet they may seem to do but little toward accomplishing it, and have but little. I say unto you that which man would bring forth into their world, should he lay it down, another will take it up. Therefore, the plan of God is perfect. It is the plan of man that is imperfect, for if the plan of man should not be fulfilled or finished, another will fulfill it. One man does not start to erect a building, and, if he should leave it half done, that another man does not come and finish it, so it can be used. Surely you understand. It is but an analogy. An analogy we would say that our own

Beloved spoke of, for He spoke in parables for the understanding of man. He could not give them the truth, for they would not understand or accept; therefore, He spoke in parables for their understanding. He said unto man that which I do you may also do even greater, but I say unto you greater things can you do also for He foresaw what he had.

BURDENS

THIS HAS BEEN BUT A PREPARATION for the burdens that are to come, so for the work that is to come was the burden necessary. Responsibilities cause growth and the growth spiritually is great, but the great spiritual growth is needful. In doing this work and the work that is to come, it shall come forth in many avenues. It will not be expressed in one channel, the channels are several—the main stream is one. There are many channels and they will be made manifest in many ways, even as spoken of in that Book, the Bible. The spirits are given to several, but the spirit is one, the spirit of prophecies, the spirit of tongues. You will find that these will be made manifest, many into one channel. This also has long been planned and planned in many lives, for only that which has been accomplished is accumulated and brought forth. What you accomplish and earn in this life you carry and bring forth in other lives. Those who work to establish themselves with the spirit, perpetuate themselves, regenerate themselves and are born again, bringing the spirit with them and the work becomes one.

You see the momentum of the spiritual, that growth does not diminish. You have brought a great momentum, a great growth, and you shall not only release it within this life time, but shall carry it and bring it forth even greater in the next, for there shall be many life times to come yet. Man trembles and says the end of the world has come. Don't believe it! The end is not here as yet. The end of the world as he speaks of it may mean the end of his own little world, but the world as a whole, no; for God that created all things and sees that which is to diminish and can see that which is to grow and be sustained. I say unto you though there will be wars and rumors of wars, and, though there be chaotic chaoses, though there be upheavals of nature, the end has not come. Each man is a world within himself; each man can destroy his own world, and that world will not come to an end.

Come! bring me your burdens, heap on my shoulders your troubles, lay at my feet your problems and leave all with me; yea! you who are overladen and weary, come unto me and I will give you rest. In the coming and in the leaving of your burdens, you must remember not to take them up again and carry them away. Often this is what is done. The coming with the burdens are there, but in the going often man takes up all his burdens and leaves them not at his feet.

It was in this wise that Moses spake unto the children of Israel and said unto them: "Bring me your fatted calf and your coat for a burnt offering, and into this offering will be heaped your sins, your problems, and, in the burning they will disappear, and in the burning they are gone forever." In this wise the mind of man was able to see in actuality the burning of his sins and problems in his level of development of the thought that was necessary for him to lay aside his burdens. Often this ritual still takes place in your churches. The burning of the candle, the burning of the incense, and the confession of the souls are the rituals. He who learns to take his burdens to the Master, himself, and leaves them, greater is his expansion and growth. He has learned to find the way through his own being, and therefore, is the greater in strength, expansion and growth in an example of faith to his brethren. These words are easy I know and simple for me to say to you, but in the difficulty lie the workings of them. Even as a child learns to perform a task in the performance time and time again, he finds it is in the performance time and time again that he learns and finds it no longer difficult, that it has become a simple thing and so learns to leave all his problems and his burdens and does not take them up again.

CHARACTER OF INSTRUMENT

I HAVE MANY WORKERS. I have many, and they are known and unknown to their fellow men. They live even as their fellow men, yet they are my people and are doing my work. The difference is noticed in their manner of speech and the kindliness of their nature in the understanding of their fellow beings. They do not partake of the things of the world and yet they live in the world. They are even as a friend or neighbor, or a stranger to be passed by in the street unnoticed and thought of only as another human being. It is needful for the silence and for the silent worker, for the silent worker accomplishes much, yet it is needful for the worker also who works in the field and is known. This too accomplishes and yet each, the silent and the known, are hand in hand for the common purpose, for the goal is the enlightenment of this planet, the upliftment of the soul.

This is not a thing confined to one race, one country, or one nationality. It is not confined to one life cycle or one generation. Each has its own workings and each contribute to the whole. Mark you well my words!

They who are chosen are not chosen unwisely, but they also must endure, yea! even longer than it would seem the strength can endure, but the strength is thereby fortified and not weakened. Look into lives of other men who have been chosen and see the years of preparation for their service, and, even in the preparation, did they render service also. Yes, this preparation began at the moment of birth, and I say that soon the time will be at hand.

COMMUNION WITH EARTHLINGS IN ITS WORKING

WE HAVE GATHERED TODAY in the search for truth and in the search for light. In the search of truth and light, we seek to find and to identify ourselves with that which has created us and brought us into being. In our search for this self, man has sought for centuries to return unto that which he came forth from in the beginning, for in his former estate did he walk with his Creator, did he have communion with his Creator and did he know himself as being a co-creator in the beginning of his days. In this former estate of being man he knew all things, and in all things, so knowing, was he in his fullness of his glory, and man came forth and did inhabit and did inherit the earth.

I have come speaking of the former estate of man and his search for the glory that was his, for the knowledge of his being that was his, and man has searched continuously. No matter where his leanings and learnings have taken him he has not found his satisfaction. He has not found that oneness and so man searches and through many forms of worshipping, through many forms of teachings seeks he this wisdom, but I have come to you dearly beloveds to say unto you, "Behold! the threshholds upon which you now stand."

Do not turn aside, for just beyond within the grasp is that which you have been seeking, and, because of your choice and of your seekings, have many things come into your lives, and have come into your lives even as a consuming fire, consuming you, bringing you to this estate of being to prepare you for that which is yet to come. All who chooses this path of learning are spared not the fire that burns and consumes, for you must walk through the flame and be touched not, and only they who have been consumed and cleansed can walk through the fire and the flame and be touched not.

I come to tell you that in the days to come many lives will be touched and come into yours, and I say that now within you are you able to receive them and be not touched by them, for man must learn not to be touched by others, and yet he must have complete compassion and capacity to love, and pour love without confusion. Herein lies the barriers of confusion—to give freely of spirit's love and in the giving know no barriers.

This force must be generated within the earth instrument (a medium). It is stored for future use and when used, will be replaced in abundant quality and quantity. This electrical force field becomes so charged that you become the instrument, or battery, of this energy. If you keep your electric force field in prime operating condition this force field can be recharged with a greater capacity and kept in better operating condition. It is then that the force field will be charged with the utmost capacity to hold the power and go forth through the instrument. Each member of a physical being is part of an instrument, each part has its own meaning and its own purpose. There is a central sun in each part of the physical being that generates a force or energy, and when each part is brought into completeness with others, then is this force so magnified, so magnetized that its use is beyond the understanding of man in his scientific endeavors. Only when man brings this science and religion together into a unified unit of one will he discover the power that is his, that he enjoyed with his creator.

I would charge you to look beyond the human. I would charge you to see beyond the appearance of others, for you will see that from you goes forth threads, weavings and catching hold to threads of others, and forming a triangular form of connection. These threads of yours are interwoven with the threads of others, and it is from these that the power and force are thus generated to a higher degree in bringing forth into togetherness with those who have learned control of their force fields and the ability to project this force to others. It then forms a base of operation that the power may flow forth in greater abundance.

Remember always the physical being is but the instrument of the power, and the power is always greater than the instrument, for even as the generator will not function without the force and power of electricity, the electricity is existing and has its power without generators. The generators then harnesses the power, but the generator must be strong in order to harness the greater power in its use in being brought forth.

Surely you can see the simplicity of this as I speak, for a small machinery used in small areas can but sustain the small areas wherein it lies, the larger piece may then sustain a greater amount of power and in a great area find its use.

When the instrument has been chosen, the path of that being is not simplified. It is then complicated for its own betterment that it may function in a better use, and that it may become the power that it has sought in the beginning to become in its use and in its service.

I feel sure that this day you understand my words and are beginning to glimpse the whole of the picture and see the pattern as it has unrolled over the time of your being. I think that you see and behold the force that even now is pouring forth from this being, for it accumulates the greater force that it shall sustain and keep with it, and shall in turn help the force to gather and grow for that day that it will be needful as a most powerful piece of a generator machinery known as the physical being. It is the use of this power, and you shall see the power in its use at far distances of the being itself, for the task of learning the discipline to project this power is needful at this time.

In the use of the mind, which in itself is an instrument, and in itself a generator of the energies collected. It is the directing part of the generator. It is the use of the mind force concentrated upon an object be it movable or immovable. You will see the effects of the generated power gaining in strength and the discipline of the projection.

Within this being has been established the power that has been necessary, but the physical and the nervous system can sustain only to a certain degree the network wherein the power is generated. This network must be strengthened and watched with care that no part of the physical being be stressed beyond its capacity of endurance of this power.

COMPASSION

How many understand compassion? It is the knowledge gained by experience in knowing that which another is experiencing. They who have not experienced either joy or sorrow cannot know the true depth of feeling in that one who is experiencing either joy or sorrow. He, who was the greatest of us, had compassion of all things; yes, even when he beheld the city he wept over it and knew that it would crucify him to his death, yet forgave it. How few in speaking the words "precious blood" understand the true meaning of the words, "by his blood;" yes, this in itself is a lesson in understanding the truth of the system of the blood and its transmutation in its rate of vibration. It is a discourse that I shall not pursue at this time.

I have spoken to you on the rate of vibration in love and the true concepts of compassion. I speak to you in praying, in so decreeing, call upon us that we may also bless and help. In sending forth your words acknowledge them into our use. Only in this acknowledgement can then the greater power be released.

DIVINITY

IT IS GIVEN TO YOU to understand the human side of man and the divine, for as often as man seeks to become the divine, the human enters in. It is the human that discolors the purity of the divine. In this wise is the true meaning of adultering. The divine is pure and as it expresses through man, the adulterating is in the human, for it is the human expressing the divine.

BEHOLD! the light as it passes through the prism. It is broken into many nonces and colors. It is the purity of these colors, according to the degree that man expresses his divinity. In all men is the divinity, but not all men express it in its purity. Magnify the good in all, bless the good in all, knowing that all eventually evolve to that state of divinity and perfection even as you. Therefore, know that he judged no man, but His judgment was just, for it was divine.

EARTH'S NATURE

THERE IS NOT ONLY TURMOIL and chaos in the world, but in human beings also. It is the struggle of the soul with the body. It is the struggle of the minds to be free. This generates a great power, and it is reflected within nature itself; there is a great adjusting period now, and a balancing. You will witness many things and many things you will see beyond the human comprehension of them, for you have the understanding, and you will behold with the spirit the truth in them. Many will question as to these things happening, many will question your faith and many will question what you believe. Remember! it is not necessary to prove God nor to reveal the inner light and truth that you carry, nor is it necessary for you to express your conviction, for in attempting these things, it is but giving meat to the vultures. That which the world knows not of, it cannot touch or destroy.

The physical form is but the outer manifestation of thought and feeling. It is the physical evidence, the visible evidence of the invisible. It is the opportunity and experience of life in the manifested form. For the soul it is good, and it is a privilege sought by many. All through the experience of life does the soul evolve and is given the opportunity to perfect; therefore, many souls must seek the experience of life to perfect and become perfect, even as their Father is perfect.

He said a little child shall lead them. The wisdom of man is foolishness in the eyes of God, and they whom God chooses to be the wise are foolish in the eyes of man. A paradox.

Let there be no doubts within you, for no matter how the world appears to you, no matter how you appear to the world, you know within yourself that this is your path. None can take it away.

I see you have been reaching out with your thoughts and you have wondered the nature of this universe, and you have wondered the many avenues of thought and truth that is your light. As it is expressed through the prism of man's minds it is diffused in many ways and often times into many colors. It is for each to seek the source of that truth that he may receive it within his own self in the pure form. This is not new for you. You have pondered at these things that you write. You have found the same thing many times; often same words used, or even different phraseology, but same meaning. This is necessary for it is a training period. It is development toward that goal of full understanding and knowledge to be received. It is what you call basic training. Yes, it is the preparation. You each have had training in different ways for same thing. Now the training is more intensified for each, even as the child must first go to a lower school before he is ready to go to a higher school. This is the preparation for the higher schools as well.

Man must learn his true relation with the universe, with nature around him, with the man that dwells within, and the god that one day he will become. When the thoughts of the daily life and of the world besiege you, my council is to lift the mind above these things, set them aside, lift your eyes, and behold the earth and the world thereof, and know that it was found good. Contemplate it! Then take up the thoughts and find that they are as nothing, and have become solved while you thought of other things. It is in the lifting of the thought, in meditation of the oneness of God, in the knowledge that all things are possible, that he who dwells within, above and around you, holds all things secure; and that the daily problems and struggles are but a lesson in many ways and often needful in the use of the training program of another.

I have looked from the mountain tops, and I have beheld nature as a sleeping giant who is awakening and even now rises and shakes a tousled head and spreads forth her arms. I have beheld the waters of this planet and the secrets within them, and I have looked within the mountains and have beheld the secrets that they too keep. I have looked deep within the very innermost beings of the earth and have read their secrets. I have beheld that which is in the inner and that which is in the outer, and I have seen, and I have rejoiced, as well as wept.

Behold! and see your planet as a flaming sun, for it one day will be a sun. Behold it! Cover it in light! and look upon it as the purity of the purple, for its destiny is indeed a divine one. Its growth is needful, for it is indeed in a sistership with Venus.

Man who measures time, man who measures light, and measures it in years and in miles does not know that he can overcome time and distance, the speed of light. The speed of light is even as the thought of the heart. We work in harmony with the light, but mankind has yet to evolve into his higher mental states, for in himself he sees only himself and cannot expand or comprehend that which is beyond his own planet and his own universe. It is vast.

Each universe is a step. Each evolves toward perfection. Each has its own guides and mentors. Each has its own messiahs. The light that pours in is of many hues, but the source of it is one. That which becomes the pure white light is one with all light.

Even now the forces are in movement, and there will be many things that will come about, and they will come not slowly, but they will tumble one onto the other, even as the stone tumbles from the mountain top and loosens the stones in their descent and soon becomes a great calamity of stones rolling, and with the power and the force hitting the valley floor will these forces also strike. It will not be but in the lives of one or two, but in many, and it will not be confined to one area, but many, for it is a time of awakening that has been needful but ignored. This may come in many forms, in many lives, for each one is a part of the whole, and the whole is aware of the lack of each part. It is also aware of the method best used to eliminate the lack in that part that it may best serve the purpose of the whole, so speak for your awareness and your perception of these things. You shall not be without knowing, and you shall not be without understanding, for these days you walk in spirit and in awareness of doing so. Perhaps I should elaborate upon the term of walking in spirit for all walk in spirit. There is not one who walks not in spirit.

In speaking of the force or the power, it is that which you have created and built. It is that which you have raised up as a temple and that which you have built and that is indeed a glory. It is a vast temple where in you may dwell. You walk in much spirit, for even the meager and the poorest are not without spirit, but according to their building is also according to their spirit. Only as man becomes determined to build and to create and to bring forth does he open the vastness of the heaven through his own desire and will to do it; or else he will deny spirit and say, "Nae! Nae! I believe it not" and in turn will he also be denied, but he who denys, denys himself. Remember this!

The things of the world that nature has done in protest is only beginning, *only*. That which man has done he has done to his ownself. Many people are afraid. Many people wonder and ask why these things happen, but not until man cries out, "Father, why, Father, deliver," then will they know and understand, and it will be only when man comes unto his knees. Yes, there is protection for they who work and serve spirit. Many will be warned of safety steps to take, but many will be led in way of good being as coming from spirit, yet there will be those who will not heed their warnings from spirit. In their own mind they will feel safe in all things. They will not be able to see that spirit sees what is needed and too late they cannot save them.

Question not my daughters! — know that man being good to his children, though he commit evil, your Father in Heaven who is greater than man how much more good would he give unto his children. Within each is the divine spark, within each is the Infinite Father and ultimately each shall find and shall know the Father within them. I say to you in this capacity have you beheld that the way of the world is what is the fear in the forthcoming and must be overcome, and, have you not been told to hold steadfast in your faith of this thing, for the fear of the world shall be overcome, and it shall be done and soon. Even now is the struggle great and the decision is close at hand, for each man faces within him the decision of either the will of God or the will of man, but I say to you behold the need as being now. You live within the "now," not that which is past, not that which is yet to be, but in the present, the nowness of time and life. Therefore, behold all things as "now." Did not my brother say unto them—"Behold the fields," and they looked unto them and they were barren. He said to behold them as they blossom and bring forth fruit. Behold it as now and not four months hence, nor the time of the season for the blossoming of the fruit, but behold this as being within the nowness of time and accomplished.

EGO

IN MAN'S STUBBORNNESS to be the one in command of every situation, regardless of where or what it is, he manifests his ego. Man cries many times and feels lost many times, yet in his stubbornness of wanting to be in full control, he blocks the things of the spirit, the things of truth and the things of love. Once it is learned that one must serve, even as the servant, before he can be the master; in your wise the discipline of knowing how to take an order that one will have then the capacity to give the order.

It is necessary to broaden the horizons of the mind in order to receive the greater truths. When thoughts are channelled into the small and narrow channels of vision and thinking, one is not ready to receive the great rivers of thought of the universal mind. To tap that source you seek, you must be willing to sacrifice much of the material world and the material thinking, for man's wisdom is foolishness in the eyes of God, and as we know our vision is foolishness in the eyes of the men that dwell upon this earth's planet. It is the ego, the personality, of the outer man that dominates. In his pride he can see naught that is beyond, nor know the inner man that is within him, but when he seeks and he finds the inner man and lets that power of the source of his being express through the outer man he has overcome. He then knows he has conquered and knows that he no longer dwells in a three dimensional world, but in a seven dimensional world. It is then the scales fall from his eyes and he beholds and his ears become sensitive; wherein he can hear that which is beyond the hearing of man—mortal man. He comes to know that he dwells upon an atom that dwells within its own universe and that universe is but the smallest of many universes. Then he becomes as an infinitely sensitive instrument, or antennae, and knows that he throws his thoughts into the ethers even as the waters are thrown upon the shores, and his universe becomes his home.

FAITH

I SPEAK TO YOU NOW in the same parable form that was given by my brother. If you have faith, even as the grain of the mustard seed, and you look to yonder mountain and you say unto it, "Be removed and get thee thither," indeed the mountain shall be so moved and be moved thither as you so desire. Faith, for it is in the knowledge that the mountain can be moved—no doubt, no negativity—no thought that will deter you from the removal of that mountain. Once man has learned the power of faith, then will he also learn to be ready to be master of this universe, for only through faith can this be accomplished. Behold! now the light, for it is as a mighty column and cometh as a whirlwind. Such is the power within you and yours to use. Use it well! I bless you with it my daughters.

FEAR

MAN HAS YET TO LEARN to overcome fear, for fear is many things. It is doubts, limitations, the unknown, the ununderstood. It is fear and self pity. It is the fear in all complexities of human nature, for man has ceased to recognize that which he is. He has ceased to acknowledge the God that is within him. He ceases to recognize and to know this God power, and becomes perplexed, confused, and despairs. It is but suffering the pangs of birth as all must suffer, but in the being born are the pains forgotten.

FOOTSTOOL

THUS SAITH THE LORD, the heaven is my throne, and the earth is my footstool: where is the house that ye build unto me? and where is the place of my rest? Isaiah 66, Vs. 1.

The earth is often referred to as the footstool of the heavens. Which is greater, the throne or the footstool?

FORCE

KNOW YOU NOT THAT EACH one who endeavors to be a contact for the spirit to flow through, the conductor, so to speak, of the force and power; has no control of the force or power, for it is greater than the conductor, but the conductor has the power to either be or not to be.

I say unto you no dam can be built to hold back the flood tide of the spirit. As a consequence has its consequence, every action its reaction, every force put into motion receives a like force. In these times are many who seek understanding and the various ways of seeking are not always understood. There is a complete turn around within the framework, but even out of chaos comes peace, out of evil comes good, out of darkness comes light; within the chaos and the turmoil I would that man need be love and light. I would say that though all could crumble about you, stand firm, hold fast, though you grasp not the understanding of many things yet know that I am with you.

FORGIVENESS

I HAVE HEARD THE CRIES of that one whose pain is great and who has that darkness in the heart and soul, and, because of the loneliness within, my heart and soul has wept, and they have bled in her anguish too. In humanness I wept with that one. Man does not know how he can crucify, but I have seen and witnessed it; and it has not ceased to be. It is a daily thing. How the soul weeps and cries out, but I say unto you, you must do even as he said, "Forgive them for they know not what they do," and even you must learn to say, "Father, forgive them," even though you know they know not what they do. Greater is their pain and anguish and greater will their sorrow be knowing this. It is then an easier thing to do in saying, "Father forgive them."

FUTURE

MAN SHALL REACH that period when civilizations shall fall, even as they have fallen in the past, but man shall rebuild and within the framework of the perfect cut stone, he shall build with the spirit knowledge that he has been given and truly in the light that has been given unto man in centuries past. The building shall be culminated into one bond, in a scroll. The scrolls of heaven that you have heard of has since been broken and shall not be sealed again. They shall come forth, but not as man visualizes them. Nae! those are the symbols of things to come, and he who has understanding shall understand, he who has ears to hear shall hear, and he who has the eyes to perceive shall behold. Man has been told to cast not their pearls before swine lest they turn and rend him, for man in his ignorance would destroy what he understands not. Has it not been said in my Father's house are many mansions? Has it not been said within me is the kingdom of Heaven? You cannot storm the gates of heaven and find them open, but you must open the gates of heaven with your own being, your own spiritual vision.

GIFT

YOU HAVE READ within the book of Holy Scriptures—"The spirit is one, the gifts are many." Unto one is given one gift; unto another still yet a different gift, yet all of the one spirit—not many. The spirit is not divided, but man would divide it. No man can be a schism. He must be all.

HEALTH AND HEALING

WHEN YOU DECREE HEALTH and healing, you decree life, for this is healing. This is health. Life is the most precious of gifts.

The hand is a sensitive center, and you can direct healing through the hand. Light is the most powerful force to be used in healing, in blessing, and in harmonizing. When you spread forth your hands in blessing, whether it be a physical act or a spiritual one, direct the light of love and blessings, and, within you, you will behold the light that goes forth. It is often of a very intense blue, next to the shading of pure white. I do not speak of a dark color, using your word intense. I speak of it in its highest color which is next to white. You would call this pale, but in reality it is in its highest intensity. It is what you term electricity. You have developed a capacity that you can use this healing force. You are charged to use it well, use it in love, in trust, and to the service of your God.

Man suffers many ills. Man suffers many gross effects, for he understands not that he must become love and light, which is perfection, which is health for his physical being. Tension from worry, consciously or otherwise, causes many of man's illnesses, and when he has learned to control the things of the mind and the emotional fields of his body, his physical being will reflect the health of the inner through the outer.

Many seek healing. Many more will seek it. Many have received it, but only through the reception of their ownselves. Man can receive only to the degrees of his sensitivity to receive. Many times he is his own obstacle and his mind blocks the flow that is given unto him. He must be completely in one with the transmitter. The one getting healing must concentrate the thought of the mind in oneness with the transmitter. It could be done through prayer or through an object you could give them for a point of concentration. An object will aid greatly in receiving the healing. Man often has not the strength within himself to concentrate in that oneness, but sits in waiting for the phenomena of it to take place instantly. He sits either in idle words, or he sits waiting for a manifestation and doubts when it takes not the place he considers it to take.

Weigh my words, ponder on them, and you will have guidance in giving healing and a method will evolve from them. This is necessary for many, but there are those with whom you deal that a point of concentration is not a necessity. An amulet was used by the ancients in their healing. It held the attention and the belief of the human mind, and many wore it upon their persons, for it gave them the belief of knowing they received.

HILLS OF GALILEE

YOU HAVE STOOD on the hills of Galilee and you have beheld many things. You have wept, you have prayed, you have held out your arms in supplication and you have cried, "Father, forgive them, for they know not what they do," even as he cried, so cried you. The Father harkened and listened to thy words. There will come many times in the days to come that your heart will repeat over these same words, and for they whom you have said, "Forgive them," may not know where they have received their strength, but it shall be given because you have said, "Forgive them." In truth you know that they do not know, and you have read, "He who sins in ignorance sins not, for he knows not that he sins, but he who sins in wisdom knows that he sins." Therefore, pray for the ignorant, as well as for the wise, knowing that they who know not will one day know, and in the fullness of their knowing will the dawn of truth of their past be revealed unto them. No greater pain can a man know than this thing, and he who can forgive is also forgiven.

HUMILITY

I GREET YOU WITH LIGHT. I greet you with love. I greet you with the open arm of spirit, for they who gather together enter within the inner sanctuary to worship God, the creator of all, to give thanksgiving and to seek blessings with all others that seek with the true humility of a humble heart. All things done in light and love, and in the true humility of the humble heart—where in is the belief of all things possible of the Infinite Father, are all things possible to be done unto you and through you. Look! Look well! even into the small and insignificant things of life. In each is a planned thing, for in many are there joy and gladness of the heart and much to be unfolded and to be learned, even though they seem the simplest of things that the heart of a child would know. I speak with words of love, and I speak with words of joy, joy in that which I behold, joy which you have accomplished, joy in that which I behold in the inner beings. Know you not what a great thing this is and what a blessed thing? Know you not how it is rejoiced in?

I speak again in the words "be comforted," for all that has been in the knowledge that naught is lost and all things to be gained. That which is overcome need not be overcome again and that which lies ahead is much of joy, much of good, for only the weary traveler knows the depths of gratitude when on the road he finds himself thirsty, tired, hungry, wherein that one comes his way offers him food, water, and a soft place to lie down to ease his weariness. Truly within does he know the depth of gratitude for these things, even as those who travel this pathway, even as you know within the depths of your beings the gratitude of the soul. Only the humble know. Only the grateful understands, but they who have not known these things know not the depths that belong to them also, for in here is the strength tested and is the weakness overcome and consumed.

In many things that man terms as weaknesses will therein lie the greatest of strength. So many hold Him for the example of life and that which He taught them—honor, reverence, but so often are a lip service only. It is often only a few who give of the heart and fewer yet who live the life. It is easier to live the ways of the world than it is to live the ways of spirit, and yet once you have learned to live the ways of the spirit, is it far the easier and far more rewarding. The ways of the world but lead to pits of darkness and the ways of the spirit lead to the heights of heaven and light. The forces of man grow great and would render him. You must stand steadfast though those about you may waiver, but I say unto you is the bright hope promised and is the future secure, for as I have told you, your well being and safe keeping have been given to spirit.

INSTRUMENTS

TO BECOME AN INSTRUMENT for God is not for the weak. Often the instruments go through great tribulations. However, no burden is given to a greater capacity than one is able to bear, for the teacher watches most carefully. In the training the strength is known, the weaknesses are known, and it is the weaknesses that must be made strong. This is not understood by the world, but only by the spirit, for it is the thing of the spirit.

Once a channel has been chosen and has complete giving to spirit, it undergoes a vigorous training. Often the reason is kept obscure from the understanding of the one going through the training. It is the necessity of the overcoming in the thought process, in the purifying, and, in the final analysis of it, the understanding is given. Many are the instruments chosen in training program of but one channel. Blessed are they who are chosen, for they too will rejoice in the fruits of their labor and the final product.

The one chosen may be as much a child and comprehend not the ways of man. This is a necessary quality, for comprehending only the ways of man, the ways of God are lost. Man loses them, and it is only in a slow process that he regains that which he has lost. God forsakes not man, but man forsakes God, for in taking the human thought and dwelling upon the things of the world, his heart is hardened;

his eyes are blinded; and his ears are deafened; and seeing, he cannot see; and in hearing, he cannot hear; and in seeking of all his wisdom, he has not understanding.

God cannot use a man of the world, for he is deadened to God's feeling and thought, but it is the simple and the seemingly unwise that God chooses and dumbfounds the wisdom of man. It is only in the purifying of the mind and soul that God is then expressed. Though man understands not these things, and therefore, crucifies that which he understands not and that which he fears. I use your word "fear," for within the depths of him his soul writhes knowing that it is God he crucifies. The human obscures the soul's tormented cry against the injustice and blanks it from within and expresses only the humanness and the animalistic tendency to eliminate that which is understood not and that which it fears, knowing that the fear is the knowledge of the incriminating evidence against that soul.

Within the soul of each person is the development of many life times, many centuries, for you have walked the earth many times. Your spirit is bound to those you are around. The path you tread may seem difficult, but the way is full of light for your understanding and learning. Your mind will question many things, and it shall be the start of your preparation to meet greater responsibilities in your service to God. Much trepidation can be overcome, and you will come to know that which is truth, for they who seek God, and they who love God and are under his wings of divine love and protection, find him. You know that the world *Judges*, but not as God judges and the choice must be made of what judgment you shall take.

There are many who would cry, "I am the way, I am the truth, I am His will." They seek to deceive you; therefore, in all thy seeking, seek first of God and take that which he reveals unto you; and, in the quietness of your thoughts, you will hear his answer. Often you are spoken to through the thoughts of your mind. Often you listen. Often you disregard that which is given to you. Think you not that you are watched over? As often as you lay in the darkest hour, often in loneliness, you are not alone, and you can be aware of the guiding presence of the unseen. One day your eyes will behold in the fullness of their awakening that which is called the unseen and behold it, and rejoice.

The world lies unaware of that which takes place within you, and it is only in the unawareness of the world that lies the protection you have. If the world knew of your innermost thoughts, it would attempt to destroy them and this should not happen. You need tell no man of what is deep within. God knows all things, and you need not tell any man, for the time will come when that man shall see and behold. There must be strength in your convictions, for the world would say, "leave these things and come and learn the things of the world."

How many life times? Time is eternity. It is that which is accomplished in the nowness of time. This is the important thing. You have not been chosen without merit. You have been called by the merit which is within you. As you seek to serve and become so dedicated, it is this light atttraction that opens the way for its use to come to you. We cannot use an instrument that is not worthy, and by that worthiness is strength, faithfulness, steadfastness and love. Many say, "Father I am ready, I am willing," and yet they have not perfected themselves, and it is with compassion that we use them not until they are ready, for a strong force of power would destroy a weak instrument.

You know that your greatest trials have been your greatest blessings in the overcoming of self. You must learn that the "me" is the last, and that it is always consideration one for the other. When you seek to become an instrument, you must become like unto the one who was a christed one.

To overcome self is sometimes a very painful thing, for one must eliminate completely the "self," the personality; for even as He knelt and washed the feet of his disciples and talked to them saying, "the master serves the servant, even as the servant serves the master, for the last shall be first and the first shall be last." Only as you can humble yourself, serve with complete love, complete humbleness can you then truly become a master and be used. There can be no pride or ego. There can be only purity of love, the sincerity of service, and the knowledge that all are of one Father.

Man must know that he is the instrument through which God works. He is the channel through which the spirit flows and no matter the station or the conditions of man when he becomes the instrument and the channel, the spirit of God flows through unhampered and the work is complete. See in every beggar a king, in every slave a master, within the lowest forms of life the ultimate, the highest. These are difficult lessons for man to learn. How many, many times have you been told truth is simple, truth is pure, truth is one? Think on this thing, for whatever is good is God, whatever is true is God, whatever is beautiful is God, is truth, is love, and one is not separate from the other, and yet it is given in many forms. Think on these things, dwell within the mansions of the Father, become one with his thoughts and express Him in all things.

Man would withhold God from man. God does not withhold himself from any man, for even in the scriptures it speaks of the prodigal son, and when he returned home unto his father, the father upon seeing him yet in a great distance, ran to the son to receive him. He did not chastise nor reprimand. He did not withhold his love in his compassion, but he ran, ran swiftly, to greet his son in his return, and it was while that one was a great way off and crying out to his father for forgiveness and wanting to be reestablished in his proper place, that the father beheld him from that distance and ran unto him. Look ye among your men, how many are found with this compassion and with love would run to his brother and greet him and lift him up and restore him?

The fires burn strong and the purifying has to be completed. All dross must be consumed, the experiences of life must be consumed within the fires, the lessons learned to take only the good of each experience, to accept in complete obedience to God's will, and at no time to let self-will enter. The mind of man, no matter the diligence on its part in seeking God's will, enters in and attempts to express man's will. This must be overcome in completeness, for only God's will must reign and be expressed at all times in all things.

You are blessed in many ways, for through this instrument you have come in contact with a broader understanding, and it may take centuries yet of evolution before man can reach the understanding. That which is being prepared now will be the light for him, for it shall be ready when mankind has need of it, and shall be his torch, his truth, his way of being; and it shall be as a ladder for mankind to climb and to reach for that which is beyond man and that which is beyond the stars waiting for his evolution and discovery.

It is in the use of a developed instrument that there is protection, for that instrument has become strong, and their development is far reaching. It has become that which attracts light unto light. There are dormant periods in soul development. There are plateaus of quietness wherein it would seem the spirit is not served. The lack of service is not that the instrument is no longer being used by spirit. There are many patterns and forms that must now take place in the life stream that would strengthen, that would endow the instrument to make it of better use in service.

JEALOUSY

IN OBSERVING all your beautiful accomplishments and seeing the many things that you have gained in throwing off the yoke of jealousy, you are to be commended. Jealousy is a trait that man has always warred against—the taking of that observation that it would seem his brother had more than he had.

It is an age old habit within families where this is sibling rivalry—the parents often favoring one child over another. This produced the sparring between the siblings. There would never seem to be a ceasing of it. Many parents are not secure within themselves and consequently are not aware of the damage they do to the children—the law of cause and effect . . . Parents often are not more than children themselves, so often are the cause of the rivalry.

There is the account of the rivalry promoted in the Bible story about Jacob. This father made a favorite of his youngest son. He set up enmity among the brothers because he chose to make a special coat of many colors for his favorite, Joseph. These brothers went so far as to connive to do away with Joseph, but through the intervention of one brother they did not kill him, but they instead took his coat and threw him into a deep pit. He was picked up by a passing group of Arabs and they took him to Egypt and sold him into slavery. Joseph found favor in the king's household, and in his far sightedness he predicted the famine that would come. He saw that the graineries were filled. Jacob sent his sons into Egypt to get food and Joseph filled their sacks with grain even to the point of returning the money they had paid for the grain.

Joseph, of course was grieved when his brothers came for help knowing that His Father did help and had sent them. Of course he was remembering his brothers' treatment of him, but, the true master that he was he held his tongue and did not reveal his identity.

When they came the second time for grain he revealed who he was. Herein is a great lesson for you. Joseph could forgive them because he had the spiritual understanding to do it. How many people are big enough to forgive and give of the largess that they have to give of their supply? Joseph filled their sacks lovingly and willingly, and put in their sacks the money for the grain that he had given them.

At all levels of governments there is jealousy. Let's say it is the largest of faults in human nature—and being called the Green-eyed monster aptly describes the trait. Herein is just another trial humans are faced with, but you know it can be overcome. Families are split apart—husbands against wives, parents against children—friends against friends—brothers against brothers—sisters against sisters—principalities against principalities—rulers against rulers; you name it jealousy is a great misqualified emotion. It is often that it takes many life times to correct this human error. On your way up on the scales of human endeavor, it is to be reckoned with one time or another. All is well and secure for man shall overcome this failing even if it takes many life times.

KINGDOM OF HEAVEN

YOU HAVE BEEN TAUGHT man does not eat of bread alone, but by every word that proceedeth out of the mouth of his Father which is in heaven. Know you not the meat that you eat of? Know you not the light that sustaineth you? Within you are the living waters of life. There have been many on this earth plane who have found these waters of life and have dwelt within the light and have been as witness and borne witness to this light to all men.

They who seek the Kingdom of Heaven first, all things are added unto them. Forsaking all, you gain all. For least a man lay down his life, he cannot pick it up and live, but if a man lay down his life for me, he shall take it up and have life eternal. Understand you these words? Only as man can die to the former self and things of self, can he live in Him, for I am the door which no man shutteth. It is they who are the least in the Kingdom who are chosen to fulfill his plan.

Man must know that God is changeless, that God ***Is,*** not was, nor will be, but ***Is.*** He must understand the way to Him and the Kindom thereof. These teachings are eternal and the school master can but teach his pupils that are ready to receive that level of understanding, and wisdom that he has to give them. Only as you work with your own selves can you progress and become more prepared.

You have but to ask, and it shall be given, for thou has been told "Seek and he shall find, ask and it shall be opened to you and ye shall receive." "Command ye Me and see if I do not pour unto you a blessing greater than ye can even receive and contain, command ye Me in My name and it shall be done unto you." What a wonderful thing this is, think, know and remember! It is in the thanksgiving that you acknowledge the knowing that you have received.

Stand for that which is truth, waiver not to the right nor to the left. Man would adulterate truth. You must hold truth unadulterated. There will be many speak of His words and give of their own understanding, but he who hath understanding of Him, understandeth all things that are of Him, and need not another man's interpretation and understanding.

Patience, watch, hold fast, for no man knoweth the hour that He shall come, except by the Father revealing it to him, for no man shall tell you of these things. Even, as He said unto him, "Take up thy bed and walk, take up thy bed of unbelief, of doubt, of inward dealings, and walk; casting thy beds into the fires to be consumed and go forth glorifying the Father." Only as you set aside your own limitations are you limitless. Know ye not the Father and you are one, one with each other. This is your scepter of dominion. This is your freedom. This is your truth. Know ye the truth and the truth shall make you free.

LACK

YOU SEE LACK. There is no lack in God or spirit. There is no lack in love. Lack is only in man, but when man seeks spirit and love of God he lacks nothing. The world heaps upon that one the lack they find within their own selves, beholding not the completeness and the wholeness of that individual who has found God and spirit and is love because of these things. I say unto you the lack is within others, for they behold not, nor see it; for they look and judge another by the lack within their own beings.

What great thing is this that you have been given? It is a commission not lightly given, but only unto those found worthy. Once again I repeat, a bed of thorns, but not without roses; valleys but not without the hills; darkness but not without light; trials but not without the help; tribulations, but not without the comfort; agonies, but not without the understanding; no, not one thing without the compassion of spirit; not one thing without the understanding or the love; not one thing, for within spirit is no lack.

There is no lack within your Father's kingdom. There is no vacuum, and when you have made your Father's kingdom your kingdom, there is no lack, though the human may seem to see lack. It is the human that is looking through the eyes of the world, but behold and see through the eyes of your Father, and you will know that which you have accomplished is a great thing. Now will you see it come forth.

LAUGHTER

THERE WILL BE DAYS when seemingly there is little cause to laugh and be joyous, but I say unto you be of good cheer, find joy within the heart and being; and laugh, even when there seems naught but darkness. It is a safety valve and will relieve much pressure, but in using laughter it must be spontaneous. It must not be forced or planned, but one of spontaniety with the other and joined in freely and indulged in of necessity.

LAW OF ATTRACTION

THERE IS THE LAW of attraction that cannot be denied. The use of this law must not be violated by the attractor or the attractee. Often it is used in a manner for a personal use of the being, and man does not find the fulfillment of happiness in its contributing to the Cosmic whole for only in doing this can then the satisfaction of service rendered be found. In this must always be what you call compatibility for it is an equal giving and in one capacity equalized and balanced by another capacity. Slowly man is learning these laws and evolving in the process of the intellect, and in the use is becoming discriminatory. In the time when I was selected and chosen, it was considered an obligation of responsibility of each being to bring forth these things as an order of contribution to the whole. Only wherein is the harmony of both contributing in a like desire and understanding, the greater the force may come forth and may accomplish far greater manner of things than man dare even think of or dream.

I find the need of greater capacity herein. The balancing factor is not yet made manifest. Each must contribute, and they who lack in the contribution prolongs the workings, but no being can withhold the course of the power, nor cause it to cease to flow and manifest. No being can turn aside the tides, nor move the moon, nor stop the sun.

I come to give of my power and of my wisdom, and I place it into the pool of forces that have been gathered in unison of this work. I would hold the tongue that at the time of its use, it be used well and at the time of its silence, it speak not.

I send you from my abode the light of wisdom, the force of energy, the stamina of strength. My hand shall remain here. Recall my words that no being can turn the tide, move the moon, or stop the sun.

LIFE

MY CHILDREN, LIFE IS NOT EASY. Its burdens are many, but you have been given the secret to cast off your burdens and to be free. You have been told how to live, and how to live a life filled with joy, light and love. Did not He say to you, "I have come that your life might be full," and he meant full, not empty—fulfillment filled with joy not sorrow. This is as your lives must be, and it is as your lives shall be, for life is much as you make it your own selves.

Great is thy light and greater are thy blessings, for they who enter and walk upright shall be filled. They who serve the central flame and are consumed by it are eternal. They who bless all life are blessed by all life, for all things are intelligent life, ye, even the leaf, the blade of grass, the drop of rain.

LIGHT

KNOW YE THAT LIGHT is needful and that all that work with light must send forth that light to their brethren. In this wise is the force and power maintained within you. You must expand your own worlds, for each person is a world within themselves. In expanding know you then there are many who sit, even as you, and even as you send forth their love to mingle with yours. The greater the power created within you, the greater the magnetism is built and the more open you become to receive that which is sent to you.

Spread before you lies the earth. Visualize this light that you have created covering it from pole to pole; once encircling it, let it expand forth into the atmosphere, for in this wise you cleanse it. Now behold you the cross, the ends of this cross are open and the light flows freely. Let no man close them. Now send forth this light in a blessing of healing that it may cover all. Even as the sun and the rain, it falls upon the just and unjust. This must be done with a free heart. It is not for you to judge or condemn another, nor to withhold that which is freely given to you of your Father, for even the least of these are His. Now that you have blessed all life; it in turn will bless you, for it is a divine law. Freely ye have received, freely give and that which receives gives in return, yes, pressed down and running over.

You have learned a great lesson, for only as you cleanse yourself and free yourself from worries, anxieties, impatience, envy, all forms of self, hidden and unhidden, are you open to receive and to give forth. In giving forth it is then that you have received abundantly. You have done well. You will do better. Soon you will glimpse the jewels that you have become, for life is like unto the diamond. You make it a thing of beauty or you hide the light that is within it. The fawcetting is not easy, and only you and We behold the work that you have done with it. You know within the fullness of yourselves that which you have received. I commend you! My love enfold you eternally.

Great can be the light within, greater can it become. Have you not been told that wherein the darkness beholds the light it would overcome and extinguish that light? Have you not been told "hold steadfast" and build that wall that the sea overcometh it not and destroy the land therein? These were not idle words given. It is both desire and the will that only good dwell within and only the good to be beholden in others. The work that we do is not an idle past time, nor do we prepare an instrument to be cast aside, nor are the promises that are made by spirit not kept, for that which is promised shall be accomplished within this day. The stronger your light grows within this work, the stronger is the opposition to that work by the light within you.

That which takes place at this time, dark as though it may seem as an evil within mankind, it is these same people that will be helped most by it; for that which they commit to bring unhappiness, anguish, and sorrow within your lives will one day return and shall be a help. Yes, even as a help unto them in overcoming their own selves, for many times man learns only through the anguish of the realization of what he has committed, not only against himself but against his brethren.

Behold my brethren the light upon the horizon for it grows steady. My brethren they who seek to work with light and to work in the light must seek to do it with all of their being. Pour all energies of thought and feeling with this light and direct it in conscious-concentrated thought! In sending forth your light bless all who work with this light! Make yourself a fulcrum, a point of light! Therefore, as a station to dispense it, become strong in it? Strengthen yourselves for the days ahead! Bring yourselves into the inner resources of your strength! Do not waiver! Do not deter!

As the light grows within each one, the vibratory range is heightened and becomes more refined. The density of this earth is such that it is difficult at times to touch down from our plane, and there is need for a medium to be used in this work. The greater light that you create, the higher rate of vibration there is. It is then that we may touch down and become one with you, and work through you throughout this universe and in this world.

To each of you these truths have been given. To each of you this light has been given for your development and growth, for each of you play a part in the *divine drama*. It is not a strange part. There is much yet I must withhold from you, and yet you are on the threshold of beholding, and the eye of spirit shall reveal it to you, and no man shall tell it to you. It shall be revealed through your ownself. When you have cried out, "Father help me", know you not the help was there before the cry?

In the use of the light, command ye the light of God, and it shall serve thee well, for all that is unlike it is consumed by it. It is annihilated in the understanding that that which is less than itself is being transformed, transmuted into the higher octaves of light. In the elimination and in the dissolving can the light come forth in its glory; therefore, command ye this same light to dissolve the darkness, for it is this cloud of darkness that obscures the way for the light to come forth in its glory to enlighten.

Command your light to go forth and see it as a mighty weapon and envision it within your soul as the very armies of God, and know that it is invisible, invincible, and invulnerable. See your army march carrying your banner of light, and see it as it descends unto that place you desire it to go to annihilate all that is less than the light of God. See it go forth as a mighty victorious thing, for it is the conqueror, and the darkness shall be eliminated. See it as a joyous throng rejoicing in its victory.

This light is your mighty weapon. This is your power, though the world may see it not. It is mightier than man. It is mightier than all things man in his imagination could possibly create into the world. It surpasses, supercedes, is ultimate, for God is not mocked, though man may mock him. God is his judge. God is his compassion and mercy seat. God is divine justice in all things, though man sees it not, nor understands it, and often would see it as unjust. Every individual is judged according to that which he has done, has accomplished, has committed to the records of his life, and answereth for all things. It is through his demanding, in his seeking forgiveness for his sins, and being able to forgive others for theirs that he may find the forgiveness. Not one jot, not one tittle of the law is eliminated and all must be answered to and fulfilled. Though it may be lightened and become as a mild thing through the seeking of forgiveness, and being forgiven, but it is accounted and required. It may not be as man reckons time, but it escapes not; therefore, use the light knowing that it can be only used according to the divine will of your creator.

That which is decreed in light and love, and is decreed through God can it be used only according to God. The outcome is divine will, not the human desire of it, but according to God. That which is decreed through the over soul of man, if put into the hands of his creator, cannot be misused. It is only the human who would seek to misuse the light in a lower realm or force, and it is wherein lies the danger. They who seek to use the light only through God and in the service of God is it done through Divinity alone. In this wise is your lesson, for many know of the light and its uses, but it is to each individual to use it in the right way. They who transgress in the use of it must answer and cannot escape it.

In your time of meditation visualize the light, and let it go forth and let it cover all the earth; let it go forth into the very being and depth of this earth and see the planet as "being;" behold it as the microcosm and know it in the relation to the macrocosm! It is a miniature and man is a miniature. Behold the light as a living thing, and bless it pouring light throughout all eternity! See it as a globe of light! Extend rays of light into the outer atmospheres that they too be cleansed and know that in the atmosphere it is a living thing!

Send forth light and do not doubt the strength of your light! Send it forth knowing that it goes as a great power, and know and visualize within you all that send forth light, no matter how small or how great, see it as a great force and power! Feel it within your own being, and know it! It is the power of God that never fails and that in sending it forth, though you see not the outward physical appearance and sign, know that it accomplishes, know that it has done its good work. It is a state of knowing. How often have these words been used—"know!" "feel!" It is in the knowing that it is accomplished. It is in the thanksgiving that you acknowledge its accomplishments.

That one that you seek the light for, receives it, and he has his own awakening. When you send light and release it, and put it in our care, it is done. No matter the appearance to you, it is done. I speak not of those who are in this place, but I speak of that one in a far place to whom you send the precious love of your heart to him. Know that it is a thing to be given freely and at all times, for the mercy seat is his salvation. Have you not cried at the seat of mercy? Again I say unto you each must seek his own way. It is good for your light and your prayers and all that you have given is not in vain, for it is not lost, and, until he for whom you desire so much finds his own way, can he break through that wall. All will come unto him in the fullness of his time.

There is preparation made for another who will come into your home. Great is his light. He is also a part of the whole, and will find help and will give help, for in the receiving is the giving, and in the giving is the receiving. Each is a help one unto the other, as each is a strength one unto the other. Each link is strength, and the chain is as strong as it weakest link; therefore, each link of love and light receives love and light, and is made strong in the whole.

I rejoice, and I receive your love, and I return it a thousand fold. It blesses not only you, but it goes forth to bless all that you love and are near you. I send it forth in rays of light, light which you shall soon receive to bless you in your work.

No matter the outer appearances of the workings, all is secure in the matter of the spirit and its workings. It may not seem to be as it should, but work with it in light and love. Many are the things to contend with, and the turmoil is great, and could be greater, but work with the turmoil with light as your weapon and love as your sword, and we serve you as your army. What greater thing than this can there be? He who stands with God, though he stand alone, is a majority.

Use your light, use your love, and it shall be well. They who come to seek, they shall find. They who seek light shall receive it, but hold fast and firm to the thought of truth and light, and waiver not, for they who come waiver. There shall be an earnest seeking in some. They shall find it through you, and you shall receive much in turn from them.

LORD'S PRAYER

THOU HAST SPOKEN WELL, as thou hast said, "Our Father who art in heaven, hallowed be thy name, thy kingdom come, thy will be done, on earth as it is in heaven." Know you the father within you, and the heaven that is spoken of, and the earth that is spoken of; is the bidding welcome of the oversoul into the temple body. It is decreed divine will to take the place of the human will, so that truly that which is in heaven shall also be on earth.

Thou hast said, "Forgive us our trespasses, as we forgive those who trespass against us," for only as you forgive are you forgiven also. In the forgiveness is the healing power of the self. Without complete forgiveness, man holds many things within his being that is detrimental to his well being, and only as he can find it within himself to forgive, then also is he forgiven likewise.

Thou hast said, "Lead us not into temptation," but you art not led into temptation. Temptation presents itself to you in many ways, in many forms.

Thou hast said, "Deliver us from evil," and your deliverance is ever at hand, for the evil that presents itself to you, you have but to see God, good in all.

Thou hast said, "Thy kingdom come, thy will be done." Your kingdom, the kingdom of heaven is within you, the will of God from within you to be done in you as on earth by Him, the God above you, which is heaven.

Thou hast said "Glory," and only the glory of the heart and of the soul are given unto God. For in the thanksgiving is the glory you receive; is the recognition that you know that which you have asked of your Father, you have received. It is in the glory, the thanksgiving, that it is done.

For every man who crieth to the Father, crieth first as a child, for its needs, but he forgetteth to glorify the Father when his needs are supplied. It is a simple thing to give glory and thanksgiving. It is even the essence of being, for it is love.

When man seeks truth within himself, then he can behold truth in his brethren; but that which he sees within himself that is less than truth, he beholds also within his brethren. Herein lies your way of being and seeing, for as you seek perfection of thine ownself and behold perfection in thy brethren you have helped him, for you have beheld the good that is there, and this is giving strength for that good and perfection to come forth within thy brethren.

LOVE

IT IS SUCH JOY TO BEHOLD the light and love, and your Heavenly Father would gather you within His arms as a mother gathers her child and would pour forth unto you His love, His heart. It is you and those who seek to serve in love, even as you, that give so freely, so willingly, so blessedly are the things which in you we are thankful and grateful. Know you not that the love that is given is like a great cloud of light? It is the aroma of rarest spices or of the loveliest of blooms, and it is sweetness beyond the knowledge of man's knowing the sweetness and the goodness. There are many words that could be given to you, but the love that flows freely from us into your hearts, and from you to us, is the preciousness of it.

You can feel the strength of love and know the depths that are fathomless and the heights that are measureless in this love, and there are no words that can give it to you, for it can enfold you as a great light that folds about you as the solftest of silks. You can be clothed in it and enfolded in it. It is a pouring forth of this love that is the greatest blessing that one can give to another, or that one can give to his brethern, for it is this love that makes all men brethren. It is not of the blood, nor of the flesh, but it is of the spirit. It is a love that no man can give unless he has received it, but no man can know unless he has the knowledge. It is a sensation or a feeling and in truth it is an experience; and once it has been experienced it is never forgotten, and that one so touched by its fire is never the same.

Man speaks of love in many terms. It is the greater portion of his thoughts and being, and yet it is as virgin land that is yet to be discovered and known, for man has yet to know the full scope of love. Open your hearts that it may flow in as liquid fire, or that it may flow forth as a mighty ocean, knowing that every point of light in your being is filled with light, is blessed by it, for love is the sacred fire. It is the all consuming fire and ye can become keepers of the flame. Tend it well!

Love can be pain as well as joy, but it is often in the pain that the greatest joy comes forth. Look within your hearts, search it out, and you will find that which is spoken of, and you will know many things that you have questioned. You will have understanding of love. When next you say, "I love you," do not only speak it with the voice, but feel it in the entire being. As the loves fills you and goes forth, that which it goes forth to will respond, and it shall come back a thousand fold to you. You can grasp the boundless power, the limitless light, the unfailing love that can be yours.

You have been given the Golden Key of Love. It is the key that unlocks doors and opens all universes. No door can remain shut long with the use of this key. You can have the full scope of love opened for your understanding. Love does not bind, it frees; love does not chain, it blesses; and yet love is the strongest bond in all creation. Love suffers and complains not; love endures and falters not; love comforts and withholds not. Love is everything, for all things were created in love—animate and inaminate—pulsating life—the quietness—the tangible—the intangible. Love is joy in the good fortunes of others; love is gratitude of blessing received, not only for self, but for all. ***Love Is***.

As you grow you will understand the simplicity and the beauty of love. Beauty is truth and truth is beauty, and both are simplicity. A great lesson is contained in one word, "Love," ***God Is Love***. I enfold you with my love, and I give thanks and praise and joy for your love.

Hold fast, remain true, waiver not, and know that we are ever with you. We are but a thought away and we love you.

Know you not that love is eternal? Know you not that it spans centuries, life times? Know you not that it cannot be lost, cannot be stolen, and cannot be destroyed? Rust and mold cannot touch it, for it is pure, shining and clear.

As each one overcomes with love the greater love they have within them, the more power they will receive. Love is the greatest thing. It is the most powerful thing, and the most transcendental thing. It is the common denominator of all things, for it is the purest light. ***It Is God***.

Yes, love has no depth, for it is depthless; no height, for it is heightless; no width, for it is widthless. It cannot be measured, for it is all, and I bless you with this love.

Love is a power and the greater the love, the greater the power and greater the overcoming of all the undesirable traits within the ego of human personality. Love is the equalizer, and it brings all things into their proper place and develops into that which it was meant to be. It is the fullness of this love that your teacher loves you.

I see that we have gathered here this morning in further search of truth, in further search of light, and in further expansion of the soul through love. Love is the expansion of the soul; for only as man experiences and knows love, does the soul expand its growth and development through the experiences of the emotions; which in turn influences the thinking and in turn is influenced by the thinking. If it be joy and happiness, which are the higher forms of expressions of the soul and are deep emotional factors also, growth is promoted. The deepest love in its purest form is a shared emotional love by two or more.

It is the perplexity of situations that cause the heart to search within itself for the failures, or the lack, and search its soul for the knowledge of these things. There is no lack in love, but there is lack in self. It may not be the individual who is searching that has the lack, but in the individual with whom they are associated with, but nevertheless, the lack is in self of the individual and not in love.

What is this thing that man seeks and calls in the term of his thinking "love?" ***Love Is,*** and man's whole being is created in love, man's whole life is in love and all that deviates from it is not of it and yet love is secure for it. All things must be done and accomplished through the highest rate of vibration which is love. All things in their accomplishment of the smallest task to the greater ones must be done within the concept of love, not only in thinking, but in the feeling, for the feeling leaves its mark upon all objects inaminate and animated. Each one leaves a trail on everything he is in contact with, and they who have the ability to read these things through the sense of touch or sight know of that person, even to his living and thinking. It is the vibration belonging to the individual and all things qualifying it by love and by the individual are these things then brought forth into the true state of its being.

MATERIALITY

MAN ASPIRES TO THE WISDOM of the ancients and the knowledge that was given, yet in doing so there lurks within the self the secret greed of mankind. Knowing these things, they therefore, are given only to those who are prepared to receive them; only to those whom they know will use them with spiritual value; only to those that they know will bring forth divine will to glorify God, not self, nor spirit. Spirit seeks not glory for itself, but seeks only to glorify the Infinite Father in all things.

Work from our planes is not understood by man, for it is an interplay in many things, but it is done through complete giving and unselfishness. It is done for the common good and for the cause of God. It is knowledge that in order to be a master one must serve, and in order to be a servant one must be one; therefore, know that there is complete compassion and understanding in your undertakings, for all have worked through the medium and the limitation of the human being—mental, physical and spiritual. The overcoming of these limitations is man's ability, capability and possibility of self mastery, the overcoming of the human and worldly things of self, and replacing them with the spiritual values and becoming an instrument reflecting the inner quality through the outer covering.

Yes, I have said I would speak of things of the world and of the material. Things in the world would seem quiet at this moment of speaking, but they are not so. There is restlessness, and it is a growing force. It feeds upon the negativity of man's thinking and feeling and the pressure of it breaks out even as the volcano, for the volcano in its pressures erupts also. There are many eruptions. I look upon this small land (Panama), and I see dark clouds. There will be a space of time where all will seem quiet and there will be a space of time for those in preparation of things, but again the clouds will gather more darkness and this land shall abort. There are other small lands and they lay and watch, even as the animal will lay and watch its prey, and absorb its actions and observe whether or not it is worthy to be left to stand on its own.

The spirit of the people feel the oppression and tension of the darker forces and rebel within their spirits and within their souls. They will rise and cry for freedom from oppression. You have been told that it shall be likened unto the days when there was a Herod, and it shall be once again, and even as it was in those days, shall it be again. Mistake not what you call symbolism and understand it for what it is. Reflect and let the mind bring the truth of it unto you.

MIND

I SPEAK TO YOU ALSO THIS DAY to lift the mind and free it, free it from its earthliness, free it from the confines you put upon it. Let it reach out beyond the spheres of man and his universe. Let it be suspended without man's thought and let it receive the thoughts of God. Contain them and in the receiving of the thoughts, you have but to ask with a sincere heart of Christ if they be true or false. Falsidity and the lie are of man and not of God, and, in the sincerity of seeking the truth, He shall reveal them to you through your own God presence. Yes, it is the ability to be as you would call impersonal and detach your ownself from all things and to look upon them in an impersonal detachment. It is separating the worldly things from the spiritual and comprehending them in their realities. This is not a lack of compassion or a lack of love, it is a state of being that will comprehend because of compassion and love. You are to recognize each man as accountable of his own self.

Each man is of the Father, even likening him unto the hand or the foot. It is part of the whole, even as each member of the physical body is a part of the whole body, even as man is a part of the whole spirit of God. The earth is looked not upon as many, but is looked upon as one, for all are of the one spirit. When man recognizes this truth and understands it, he can recognize his brother as a part of the whole spirit, even as he, and know that God is not found in complexities, but in simplicities, then will man eliminate and be delivered from what he calls disease.

There are many things I would say unto you and many things I would tell you of, but man has yet to develop his understanding and his capacity to receive. In the taking of these things, I repeat do not take them in the sense of personal, but impersonal; and then in the understanding of them, apply them to the personal. The analytical mind must not only analyze them for comprehension, but upon the reasoning of the understanding. Apply it also for the growth of the soul. I speak not words to pamper or to mollycoddle, but I speak truth that man can be man and accept that which is given to him for his betterment and his growth.

The mind of man is now going through and into its evolutionary stages of development. His physical being, having developed to this phase, will continue in its form, but the mind of man must now develop that it too may attain its proper stage and form. The state of its being at this time is a small thing at the low level. I speak of it in terms of a child who is in a kindergarden being prepared for a higher level of education and training. Man uses a small portion of the brain, which, in itself, is the finest instrument known in the world. That which man has yet to discover of the mind of man is so far reaching and so vast as to overcome even the trained minds of the scientists of this time.

There will be one to come into this world that will dedicate his entire life span and cycle to the study and the enlightenment of the brain. This is being prepared as the guiding hand to move mankind from his present level into the paths that he has need of to use, for he has been slow in his evolutionary climb. It is through the level of the thinking mind that has detained him. In each generation there has come those who have been beyond their time in their writings, their teachings, their thoughts, and it is they who have been the hope and the light of these generations, even as the culmination of these things will be used in the future generations.

God perpares the way for his children, and when they have need of light He gives them light, for it was given before that generation was yet to be brought into expression. Even the level of your understanding and teachings will undergo a great change. There will be discontent, unrest, and deviation from the true principles. The struggle will be great, but those who have the steadfastness of the faith and the knowledge of the truth shall be victorious. It is to them that the future generations will look for the light and the enlightenment of the understanding of the mind.

I say to you to ponder those great souls of the past in your history! Follow the pattern! It is a simple thing to trace, and you will see God in action. You will understand my words more fully. There are many things that would be spoken of on this subject, but it is one. There are many.

The training of the mind is an ardent task, for it is a simple and easy way to be untrained and not thinking. Therein lies the evil and the temptations, but the mind that trains itself of good thinking, therein lies the salvation and the good. Therein lies the truth man seeks. Yes, the mind is chained in many ways. It is shaped and molded by man's thinking, by his reading, by his hearing, by his seeing, and the senses of his being to weigh that which is good and that which is not. Therefore, weigh carefully all that your senses bring to you in the thoughts of your mind, for man has many senses that he has not developed or trained, and he follows only the five senses of his physical being. There are those who have developed seven senses, but they are yet few, and it is they who must lead and guide their brethren into paths of righteousness, right thinking.

You have a mind that is discernible, use it, for there are many minds that come in touch with your own. The contact and stimulation of other minds and thinking are good, providing you weigh that which your own thinking accepts, for each one seeks though it may be as different as day and night. In your way of seeking, therefore, contribute your thoughts to others that they may think good things and open their minds to receive greater knowledge and wisdom and understanding. The only door is the door of love.

Let no man shut that door within you. You seek the answers to many things and you ponder many things, but often in the twinkling of an eye the mind receives the answer. Often in your pondering and your questioning, you block the free flow of thought that is your answer, for the mind reflects many times the answer it receives—until the thing it has sought comes into full being and manifestation.

You will find that when they who come to this home can come with an open mind, they will receive that which they seek, but a mind that is blocked with confusion of questions, demands, supplications, cannot be given these things, for that mind is as real as thy own concrete walks. It can be as a cloud, and no matter what knowledge would be given, it could not be known or accepted in its unadulterated form. Often times, such knowledge would further confuse that one who is already confused.

It is necessary that you learn to listen as a clear channel to absorb as the sponge and to take no thought until after all has been received. It is not that we withhold. No, when we withhold, it is only out of an understanding of the results to that one who would become more confused, or bring into play thoughts of other things that are in no wise meanings meant to be given.

Remember for all those that enter into your house, see the Christ light around them. This will automatically cleanse them and they will leave outside your door that which is undesirable within your home. There are many who enter here and each one brings much with them and leaves much behind. Therefore, cleanse and purify always on the leaving of each one for you have created a place of light, and the vibrations must be maintained at the highest levels. They who come seeking will receive whether it is knowable to their conscious mind or not. They who come to teach and give as well as they who come to learn and receive are equal in their work, for it is as needful for the teacher as it is for the pupil. Light is the source of being, for being comes from light, and returns to light.

You have often heard it said a little knowledge is a dangerous thing, and it is far more dangerous than you realize, for with a little knowledge man can be self-destructive, as well as attempting destruction to others. It is best in all thy knowledge and wisdom to have understanding, and it is the understanding of the sacred trust and responsibility of such knowledge. Many come seeking knowledge to further their own aims. Such knowledge as this is not for the profane, for they who seek for self and the use of self, and the conquest for self, are the profane, but they who come seeking with the sincere desire to develop a way of service, and understanding, and in love, these are the sacred ones. They must realize that all seekers are not as sincere as they, and must keep the knowledge they gain as a sacred-inviolate trust.

Be ye wise in all things, but be gentle as the dove, meek and lowly, and humble as the lamb, being as the lillies of the field. In this wise you are the Kingdom of Heaven, and all things are added unto you, for the pure in heart shall behold their God face to face and shall not die, but will have eternal life.

Many aspire to these teachings, and in aspiring to these teachings they narrow the confines of their minds. The mind must not be confined to limits. Man imposes his own limits upon his mind and its state of growth. He must accept the complete freedom of the mind in its seeking and in its growth. You have found no difficulty in projecting your thoughts to those who are at a great distance from this place who have their being, their life and their ways. It is not difficult for you to recall the memories of places you have lived prior to this place of being.

Though man may not always bring into conscious knowledge that which the mind has recorded, it is nevertheless there filed away within the brain cells of his mind and being, and in instances of need he can call forth that of which he has need.

They who have gathered here today have gathered in a learning of their own accomplishments, for they know now that in learning one must give also that which he has learned, and that it must be given the vibration of sincerity and with the whole being. This is a stumbling block in the way of man, for he perceives not nor understands not that which he receives from the Infinite must be given freely. It is not a thing to be handed unto one and denied unto another, but it is to be used with discretion. For in giving, it is given unto those who recognize its values, its uses and will apply them and use them in the correct way for the good of not only themselves but unto all.

To understand these words is to become wise and to become wise is to accept a responsibility of the knowledge that must be used in its wiseness. In being wise there are many things, including intelligence, understanding and knowing of knowledge; but the use of it, whether it is done wisely or unwisely is in the terms of which Jesus spoke. He came forth to perpetrate the truth and to give it unto all generations, and, even as in this time, was he not understood by all men, but his disciples absorbed His teachings. Being men is like unto a filter pouring the light or the substance into the filter, it is given in its pure state of being, but in the filtration is it broken into nonces and many shades and colors of truth. In the giving was it given in its pure state of being, but in the distributing of it, or in the filtering, only part of the pure state of being was received by man. It is these things you must seek to understand.

Much has been written and recorded and yet so little is known about the mind. Yes, man, who thinks he has developed his mind, finds he has a great distance yet to travel. In this wise does he falter, for in his conceit of his own ego he terms himself all wise and all knowing and limits himself to his own small sphere of thinking when he has but to reach out beyond the sphere of it, but he fears many things. He fears the censure of mankind. He fears to lose touch with reality and be thought mad. He fears that he would be thought different from another, and even now they who have dared to go beyond this sphere are held in abeyance by all men and termed as being different, odd, perculiaris, and yet within the heart of man he knows and would be that peculiar also, except for his fears.

I speak plainly for you to understand me, for I speak in using the strong power of the mind. It is a storehouse of your energies and must be kept in good working order, even as a fine and delicate instrument; even as the watchmaker keeps the watch in perfect repair so that it will run perfectly. This is called self-control and is the mastery that is sought by many. Man's power of mind is strong to rule all things and man must learn to rule self first. Only in control and mastery of self can he then learn control and mastery of all other things. This you must learn that you too, even as these who stand here may control your ray of light and control all thoughts that come to you, must have complete power over all thoughts that go from you. I would speak for you to think of these things in your meditation, and I would speak to you to bring all thoughts of your mind in front of you and be merciless in eliminating that which you know cannot help or that which you know will hinder. When a pupil understands his teacher, he has come a long way, for then he opens himself humbly and accepts what he finds. Not many, not many do this thing. Yes, I am very, very pleased with what I find, and I will come again to speak to you.

ORIENTAL vs. OCCIDENTAL

MANY WONDER AT THE WISDOM of the Oriental in its opposition to the wisdom of the Occidental, and yet the fluctuation between the two trains of thought are in actuality the same, for they seek the same and ultimately will obtain the same. One is even now in its struggle to proclaim itself, the other has long established its religion or thinking, whether you term it occidental, orthodox, unorthodox, or oriental.

The basis of man's thought is truth, and he seeks truth. The ways of man seeking are as different as the way of his thinking. As a man thinks in his heart so he is. If he thinks good he becomes and reflects that which he seeks and in so doing becomes so strong a force that he draws unto himself that which he thinks and, as Jesus taught, believing that you receive these things, you receive them. This is a secret long known and understood by the inner temples. Man believing in good and receiving good, attracts it and receives it, but the mind and thinking wherein I speak of today often becomes cluttered and collects much garbage. Man must eliminate garbage from his mind and thinking. Even as you would clean an edifice, so you must clean the mind in its thinking.

This is not an easy task for many, for they would part not with their thinking, but would hold their thought as a treasure and not see it as a collection of trash.

PATIENCE

OFTEN MAN MUST LEARN as a little child, and to the one as like a little child, I would say, "Teach thyself before teaching others." Become that which you seek before expecting others to become likewise, for only in growing can others learn to grow. There is one word needed—"patience." To one who is as a small child in perception, I say, "you hold much in you hand, but you must know what you hold, for there are times you would drop it." Hold fast to what you have. You have much. What you ask for is not easy, and it is a lesson hard to learn. I speak like a father to a child, and he says you have all things, but you do not accept you have them. He says you have great way. You must hold fast. He says, remember His brother when he would say, "Not my will Father, but thy will be done."

When you are ready you will take your place where you belong. When you no longer cry for place, but accept place then you will be ready. You must bring self in one-pointedness and be steady like a rock. You must know what you have. You have been given many visions, but you must stand back and behold and stand fast in your own self. You serve in many ways where you don't think you are serving. You must remember that a master serves, even as a servant serves a master and be willing to accept that service.

As each one grows he is drawn into another level of growth and is drawn as a magnet to that source of light. Often it is best to leave the seed in the earth for it to grow and just be the ray and the sunshine to nurture it. Do not force the seed for therein it cannot grow. Often that in which you seek to help the most and love the most would seem to reject the most. If you will give patience and love in time they will return the recognition and give back ten fold the love you have given them. It is to each individual to grow.

There is a time for all things and a season for all things. There is a time to be a child, and there is time to be an adult. There is a time for breaking and a time for mending. There is a time for parting and there is a time of coming. There is a time for stillness, even as there are times for activity. Remember and release that which you hold closest. You must learn to release that it may return and return in its fullness. This is a lesson and for some it is very hard to learn.

Many things require much patience, and in joy you would give much, but I say unto you give unto God. When man is ready, then give and share your joy! Yes, you are my beloved ones. How precious a thing! Finer than the rarest of jewels! Greater than all power that man can conceive! How infinitely precious! Know you not my love in this wise for each of you!

Patience! watch! hold fast! for no man knoweth the hour that I shall come, except by the Father revealing it to him, for no man shall tell you of these things. I say unto you, Behold! Rejoice! and be glad for your fulfillment is at hand. Even as He said unto them, "Take up thy bed and walk. I say unto you take up thy bed of unbelief, of doubt of inward dealings, and walk casting thy beds into the fires to be consumed and go forth glorifying the Father! Only as you set aside your own limitations are you limitless. Know ye not the Father and I are one, and you and I are one? Therefore, you are one with the Father. This is your scepter of dominion. This is your freedom. This is your truth. Know ye the truth and the truth shall make ye free.

PEACE

THE GREATER CALM and peace are after the harvest storm, and the outer experiences of life are the turmoils, wherein the spirit grows.

A PLACE OF LIGHT AND A PLACE OF WELCOME

I SAY UNTO YOU "WELCOME" into the Circle of Light, and I greet you with the open hand of brotherhood, for such is the greeting and for such is the welcome. When you have built a place of light and a place of welcome for the spirit, it receives the light and the blessings of spirit; even as you welcome us, we welcome you.

Always we seek to meet with those who love and have joy in their beings for us, for the gladness of the heart and the joy of the soul are as a beacon of light, and, as you learn your lessons well, you grow more confident in what you are doing and try harder to grow higher in what you are learning. In this thing is confidence even as the things of the spirit, for as you grow in the spirit and the things thereof grow also the confidence and the faith in you in spirit.

When first a child walks, it needs the guiding hand of a mother, but as confidence in his doing grows so does the ability to walk grows, and soon he walks uprightly and he walks well. These things you learned and gained confidence in as children, and they are the most important things, for only in becoming confident and becoming strong in self, comes firm belief and trust in spirit. I come to say to you—you have grown much and no longer are as little children in things of learning of spirit and trust in spirit. This is most needful, for there are always the doubts, the anxiety, the worry, and they are the things that would destroy the confidence and the faith in self.

You have been told to build a strong place in you in faith, now you have built stronger, and it has been most needful. Even as a wall is built strong to hold out the sea and keep said land back, you must be as a strong wall. There is one who says unto me "even as ship in storm." It is time then for you to be strong and to put trust in spirit for only as spirit controls the helm of the ship is it brought in safely into the harbor. This one says to you to understand this thing.

There be many on this side and even more every day added. Only as light and force of being grows and, as they grow, does it becomes as a thing much higher and reaches out, and they who be of higher realms are able then to reach you. This be thing in matter of mind, thinking; and matter of heart, feeling; for through heart is love and understanding; through mind is thinking and knowing. You are in close touch with many of these people, but there be many other people also, and, as you reach to know other people, they welcome you also. It is a simple thing when you reach out and seek help for self, then is the help given, but when one does not reach out and ask, help is not given. Help can only be given when it is asked for, yet many stand fast and wait.

I perceive you in the connecting links of thought. You seek to know of spirit and receive much knowledge in the ways of spirit, and, even as was told to you, is it now to come to pass. You have but to behold the signs of the time and to behold the fulfillment of the words that have been given. It is at the end of the race that the runner becomes most weary, and is it not most needful for stamina and courage to finish? How many have lost the race for only a few feet further?

They who seek to carry the torch of light and truth must not weary, and though the strength seems to be spent, call upon the inner resources and great is the victory.

Have I not told you the changes within the churches and religions? Have I not told you the changes within even the system of schooling?—the changes within science and within the world? Have you not seen nature in changes? Ponder on these things, for even now the threads are being gathered and the weaving has been begun, and I say to you that this weaving is in the hands of the master artist.

Look you well to the uses of the light that even science employs and find that which once was considered to be fiction in scientific things is no longer fiction, but reveals truth in reality of being. That which a few have seen in the far distant times, even now comes into its own. Even now they who have spent what they consider to be a lifetime in the study of these things, begin to learn that in the beginning of their knowledge was their knowledge of all these things.

PLATEAUS

YOU HAVE OVERCOME to the periods within your life where you have felt left without anything, and I speak of it not only in the physical, but from the standpoint of the spiritual in gaining knowledge and understanding. In the plateaus reached in spiritual development there is always the questioning, there is always the wondering, but there is also the plateau within the spiritual development where no longer are the questions or the wonderings. There is the acceptance. There is the steadfastness, and there is the trust of gaining faith without seeing, nor hearing, nor touching. It is this within which our brother spoke, believing only if thou have seen and touched and beheld, but greater are they who believe yet have not seen, nor touched, nor beheld.

There is the ability to hold to the untangibles and be fast and steadfast in faith. This works a miracle of natural law within the soul. This is indeed a final testing of your true merit and mettle. You would seek the answers to many things, but I come to speak only of the answers to spiritual things.

I speak wherein I behold the treasures of the spiritual storehouse, and I speak of the things which I behold within the realms of the soul. I speak also of a knowledge that all things are under control and that all things have an answer though the human cannot divine oft times the answer as it should be. In spirit there is the elasticity of acceptance of the divine creator in his knowledge, infinite wisdom of all things, and the knowing that the preparation before the need arises is already there.

There is the vast need for the broadening of man's mind in understanding of these things, as he has limited himself in seeking the understanding, for in seeking, he has brought to these things terms of material value. He seeks to obtain riches, but puts the earthly value of riches upon it. He seeks to gain vast knowledge, but in seeking this power stamps it with the ego of self for the use of self gain.

POLARITY

ONCE AGAIN MY DAUGHTERS are gathered together forming a triangular polarity necessary to bring forth the spirit and to bring forth the truth that you have sought. The bringing together of these most precious ones are needful to bring forth the force and the power; not that it cannot be brought forth individually, but it is done, as you well know, and you are ever increasingly aware of the spirits about you. There are the natural laws of the universe to follow and fulfill even as of the earthly laws of man to follow and fulfill.

Once in the understanding in the field of electronics there is known unto man scientific knowledge of the necessity of certain polarity magnetism, the positive and the negative, that is necessary in order to conduct the power of the unseen source into the use and manifestation of the material outcome. You comprehend me!?

Now the work you are in, you have been told, is also a part of the vastness of the whole. Many parts shall now be brought together into focus, and the several shall become one. This is necessary to reach all levels of mind and thinking that man calls conscious-states of being. Man, in his attempt to open the doors of the sub-conscious, the cosmic-consciousness, and the super-consciousness, has sought to eliminate the struggle that is far more worthy of the attaining results. He shall not completely succeed in this, but shall learn from it the necessity of the inner searching and seeking of self without the stimulation of processes known to open the way of the mind. Thus, I say, the way you have chosen is far the better for in it, though the time spent seems long and arduous, though it seems to be one of digression and not of progression, you shall accomplish the ultimate and be of the force and of the power that can bring it forth.

PRECIOUS GIFT

THERE ARE MANY HERE this morning with you, and I speak of the day in the terms of the morning light. There is one here who holds within her hand a crystal ball and her eyes are solemn and wise with wisdom beyond her years. She would speak to tell you of many things. There are many who gather at the light, and you, who love the light and serve it also, have their service. She says she has come to serve with you. It is a precious gift, the gift of love. It is the love of one spirit for another, and it is a most precious gift to you.

PREPARATION

KNOW YOU NOT THAT THE preparation of each individual is needful? Often the more strenuous preparation of the instrument overcomes much of the preparation of the instruments needed and chosen for that one final accomplishment. Liken this even unto He who was crucified for all mankind. Each one has his overcoming, but He who hung on the cross for them overcome much of their trials and tribulations. Man reveres the cross, but in his moments of reverence they are few and forgotten until the next moment of reverence. The daily application of true reverence is a *must* between man and God. How often do the Scriptures speak—"watch," "be steadfast," "keep the oil within the lamp," for no man knoweth when his Lord cometh. Man is lax in applying himself in his worship of God and keeps not the oil in his lamps, nor watches or keeps close guard for that hour.

Yes, you comprehend my words, for you have toiled greatly within the spirit. It is a commendable victory, for you have done well in leaving no stone unturned and shall remember the necessity of this in the days to come. Man is his own task master, either he is strong or he is weak, thereby the accomplishment lies in his hands, whether it be victorious or a thing that must be taken up another time.

Once you have established within you the knowledge of knowing that we are ever with you, it is then our help, our love and our light that will sustain you. This is the strength for you to go on and continue, for the overcoming is a great thing, and no man is left alone. No man is without God's love or His help, but each man must seek it, must ask for it, must make the effort for it, and must search within himself first. In knowing himself and sparing not, he knows himself, and in the overcoming are all things for him. Great is the light! Rejoice within yourself! It is a light that you have helped to build, and it is a light that you help to sustain.

In sending forth the light command it in the name of Our Lord and release it into His hands that he apply it, and the victory is sure. In the use of God's light command it in God's use, knowing that it is accomplished. I repeat the word "knowing." It is the knowing of the entire being. It is of the body, of the mind, and of the soul. It is an inner conviction knowing that which you have decreed in God's name is accomplished. The light you have sent forth to do battle with, see it in its most powerful brilliance. Know it to accomplish its purpose! Sustain it with your conscious mind and feel it with your light and love! It is a thing that you do not alone, but have the complete cooperation of all that serve the light and of all that are of the light.

In the use of the light you have assurety of knowing that it is being accomplished through God's will and not your will, knowing that your efforts and your work are added to His. It is in this wise that good is accomplished and spirit is brought closer to man.

You are all children of God and all follow the path of learning and all have the cross to bear, but also many things must be accomplished through your own selves in your learning. Therefore, I charge you to pray often.

The one you speak of struggles. The physical manifestations of her struggle has been made apparent, but yet she too must overcome self and human-thought taking and bring into control many things. Great is her power and understanding, but much is needed until the overcoming. The realization that God's will and not man's will must be dealt with must be understood completely in knowledge and acceptance. Much good is done and much light is used, but yet much must be overcome, for all the learning that has gone before has become obscured within herself and she must relearn much and bring it forth. She needs your prayers that she will find herself and come into her right state of being to accomplish God's will, according to God's way and not man's way. To decree God's will, but to employ man's will to accomplish it cannot be done. In this wise all that is to be decreed by you, decree it in God's name according to God's will. In the use of the light you have the assurety of knowing that it is being accomplished through God's will and your will and in knowing your efforts and your work are added to His. It is in this wise that good is accomplished and spirit is brought closer to man.

I speak of these things for your understanding of this child. She is a child of God and follows the path of learning and has the cross to bear, but as well many things must be accomplished through her ownself in her learning. Therefore, I charge you to pray only for her accomplishment and that it be made swiftly within herself. She has learned of the light and has good intentions in the service of that light, but often lets the human will and intention enter in. Yes, many may be hurt by letting self will enter their being, but the greatest to suffer is that one who has let this happen; therefore, the greater the need of that one. How often spirit would reach out, but man denies the hands that are reaching to him. How often God's children places the wall between them and their Father. How often does man cry out, "intercede for me," when he, himself, needs only his own intercession with his Father, but in his consciuos mind he has put the wall between him and divinity and cries out, "intercede for me" when he has only to destroy that wall that he himself built.

Yes, I would speak these words again to you and harken on to them well. Man has built of his own thinking the wall that separates him from God, and then he cries out for those of the spirit to intercede for him. He needs no intercession, but needs only to destroy or eliminate this wall of the human mind and come unto the Father and say, "Father, I come unto thee as thy son and I intercede to thee of my ownself." It is then that man will know this sonship with the Father and that he and his Father are one, but until man learns this lesson he will cry out, "intercede for me," and the spirit will intercede, for spirit has mercy and compassion on the weaknesses of man, knowing that one day he shall overcome them, and he in turn will intercede for his brother. His brother also learns that there is no barrier except the one that he, himself, places between him and his Father. How often beloved sisters have I heard the cries, "intercede for me—tear down the very gates of heaven—weep at the feet of God and carry my need to him." How often have I comforted him, and how often have I cried in mercy for him? Yes, an intercession shall be needful until man learns this lesson. Man has no need of intercession. You have but to claim that which is yours as a rightful heir, for you are no longer as a child, but as a man. To stand and to walk upright in the spirit is a great thing, and you walk with man upright in the spirit.

Within the soul of each man is development of many life times, for you have walked this earth many life times. The path of preparation may seem difficult, but it is not without its rewards and its joy. The limitations often placed on the physical being are to help shape and mold the destiny of that being. Soon you shall behold the shaping of many of these nuclei of destinies and see into the time stream of their past and know how this shaping has been done. When you begin to see these things for other beings, you are better able to behold your own being.

Know you not that to receive you must prepare the room in which to receive? You can receive only to the degree of your own sensitivity of heart to receive. As you become sensitive, the more you can receive. Many cry out and would have the gates of heaven open and flood unto them, but unless they are ready to receive it, they cannot receive it in its fullness. Only in the preparaton as he prepares himself is the capacity for the receiving.

PURPOSE

IN COMING TOGETHER for a common purpose are the coming together in adoration and worship, for the sole purpose of all things is to glorify that which has created it; and all things that are done and understood in glorifying their creator are made and found good. Yes, for within the recesses of your heart, you have been eager, and have found a certain excitement. Hold fast! for soon the time is at hand. It must be met with eagerness and with joy, for it is a gentle thing, and yet the world comprehends not its power. It surpasses all that man knows in the strength or force of power. Behold the love of spirit! Its manners and its ways are not man's ways, for it works toward good, but the good of all. It is not an easy thing for it is firm.

I speak to you for your understanding of the word "easy." It is not as thy thoughts are of it. I shall try to simplify my meaning of one small word with many. Spirit is not to be used or abused by man in any way, for it is not man's to control selfishly or for his own will, and yet it is man's for his power and for his taking; therefore it is not an easy thing in your terms of pushing or using, but it is firm and steadfast in its workings. No man can mock God, for no man can hideth the thoughts of his heart, nor thoughts of his mind. Man in scheming many things, thinks himself master of his scheming, and often the very schemes are his undoing. Unless he works for good and works with spirit, he is his own undoing; and so it is until he learns and knows and works wherein is his rightful place, and in his rightful way does he glorify his creator in all things.

I have stepped in to speak as the master builder works must his work be tempered and strengthened that it shall stand fast in all things, and so as it has been made ready, shall it stand in the final days of its being.

A SALUTATION

HELLO SISTERS! great is the light this morning and strong are the forces that are here, and I come to soothe and to bless and to pour love unto you. I bring with me the roses from His garden, and they scent the air and the softness of the petals fall upon you. I come to bear testimony of His love and to His beauty and to His truth and to His goodness. So many send you their love.

There is one who comes to bless you and bring you the silver cup and he says, "Blessed Sisters! I take communion with you, and I take communion for you, and I offer up the

Holy Sacraments for your well being, for such is my love for you."

SEEDS OF THE SPIRITUAL

IN THE PHYSICAL ARE THE SEEDS OF THE SPIRITUAL, and within the physical lies the incubator of the soul and that which the soul learns and obtains through the physical expression is its growth. Always the outer is the reflection of the inner and the physical characteristics take on the soul characteristics also, and in the face of man lies the reflection of the accomplishments of the soul. You do not put a light under a bushel to hide it, but set it upon a lamp stand that all may behold it, and so likewise does a light radiate from within you. They who have the eyes to behold it, glorify it, and they who see not feel it and are aware of it. This is the word man uses termed "radiance," though he does not behold the light, he is aware of it when he says, how radiant is this one!

No man holds the tide, no man stops the sun, no man interferes or deters the will of God. Yes, come forth! If one place closes, another opens. Spirit come forth! though man often stops spirit.

SELF—SELFLESSNESS

"SELF," THE WORD IS SIMPLE. The accomplishment is much more difficult. As you struggle and make your effort to overcome self, you receive the help that you need. It is as the Pharisee who stood in the temple and made loud his praise and much of his giving, but only until he could come quietly in the silence and secrecy of the temple, humbly serving His Father, saying his prayers within his own self, without that you call public recognition, is he then ready to step into the fullness of his own mastership. It is even then that he as our brother could stand and say, "I, of myself, can do nothing, the Father within me can do all things, for my Father and I are one."

The death of self, the life of overself, mortal into immortality, corruption into incorruption, darkness into light - what matters if the world judges a man's wealth, or intelligence or position, for the things of this world shall pass away and be as nothing. The knowledge that you are one with Him is your security. You have heard the words, "Christ is all"—simple; think! "Christ is all." Know you then that you can become "Christed" as well. When Jesus walked this earth as a man, he was a man, but when he became Christed, he was the "Christ," and said, "I, of myself, can do nothing, but the Father within me can do all things." And, have you not the Father within you?

Know you not that each soul has his own pattern and path? Each soul does not just happen, is not just carelessly thrown into its place, for many great souls have risen from what man terms "the depths." Each is placed with great care, each is placed with his potentials, each comes into his fulfillment, and yet many lives seemingly are lived fruitlessly, but that is not so. There is meaning to every life lived, no matter how meager, no matter how poor, no matter how rich. Each soul is working out its own destiny, reaping its own rewards, fulfilling its own meaning, even as you.

When you seek to help and give, you must not doubt your own self, for the doubting is, as you would say, the monkey wrench in the mechanics. Where there is not visible evidence, there should not be despair. That which you claim to be intangible is far more tangible and real than that which you call real and tangible.

It has been said continuously "man must overcome self," but how often does man critically condemn and judge his brother for the faults he, himself bears? He sees them not and would set himself to be judge over his brethren. No man can judge another least he subject himself to the same judgment. Herein lies the stumbling block to progression and soul growth, the stumbling block of the ego. The term "Self-righteous" is in itself explanatory for it applies to them who think they deal with their fellow man righteously. They set the rules and the laws themselves, but they shall fail by the same rules and laws, for they have subjugated themselves also to these things. We who judges with righteous judgment, which is of the spiritual and the judgment of the spirit, subjugates also himself to spirit and its judgment, and he shall be the overcoming and the victory, for he is judged by God and not by man. Therefore, judge with righteous judgment and judge not as man would judge. When I speak of the word "compassion" and of the word "understanding" and of all things of the spirit; yes, in the digestion of these things much will be gained. I impart them to you because of my love, and I enfold you with my thought.

It is the giving of your love and your prayers, even unto that one who would use you in a most unhappy way, for in giving love is their sucre and your salvation.

There are many levels of attainment and, in seeking the highest, it can be sought only through the control and the overcoming of the self. They who would seek the highest spiritual levels must seek them within their own being. It cannot be given by another. It cannot be gotten from another. It can be found and obtained only through the self and the overcoming into the overself. It is a search that each one can find only through their own efforts and from within their own beings. To company together, to joy together, to speak together is a blessed thing, for in it is growth also, and, in talking over many things is also growth. It is in the sharing and the giving of the gaining that others gain also, for herein lies the way to ponder and understand, and to gain also by another's experience.

It must be remembered always that you are a people set aside as having a truth that is not always readily accepted by the world. Therefore, it is necessary that you must stay within yourselves to a great extent. You cannot always share what you have, for the world understands it not, and, even as a beast of prey, would rend you asunder. This has happened so many times.

Blessed are they who are the pure of heart, for they shall see their God, and behold him in His glory. The glory is to Him and not to them, and, in this realization, it is then they glorify and seek only to glorify the Father. It is when man ceases to glorify self and seeks and glorifies the overself, the oversoul, which is the divine part of man, it is then he attains his full stature, and his scepter of dominion.

The morrow shall bring much and the days are full. Strengthen your own self, and in the strength that you, yourself, become, it is this strength likewise you can give to others, but only that which you have can you give; therefore, strengthen thine own self.

They who work together and work for good shall receive good, and they who work in the light, becomes the light. Many things shall come to pass for this is the time of great trouble and turmoil. This is the time that the black forces gather and would battle. These forces are in the thinking minds of man, whether they be for good or for evil, whether they be positive or negative. Man must battle them within himself, and he must overcome the negative with the positive. He must cast out of his own self that which is less than the good, for these are the signs of the times. It is not only of the individual, but it is of the nations, as it is of the heads of the governments, as it is within the whole of this planet.

Many are willing to serve, but cannot give of their completeness. It is as He who said in parable, there was a rich man who sought to serve and had the willingness of heart, but when required to give up his riches he could not do so. He was not willing to give the wholeness of self. This is not spoken of in terms of material wealth. This is spoken of in terms of self, and of individuals, and the riches are those that the soul has earned, yet could not give completely that which was it's own. Man does not comprehend the true meaning of these words, for he would apply them to his world and the material gleanings. These scriptures are often misinterpreted and misunderstood, for man seeks to fit them to his own level of understanding instead of lifting himself to their level of truth. These are His words to be pondered upon.

SERVICE

MAN SO OFTEN MISUNDERSTANDS the word "service." It is the true giving of self in love, divine love, whether it be in thought or word or deed. It is the outpouring of the inner through the outer. . . . You can realize in a moment of time the true meaning of this word service. Often your greater service is done in silence. The light you work with, the healing you send forth, you may not see its outer manifestation, nor behold the material result, but it is beheld in the spiritual planes and the result is great. Each has gathered here for a purpose, but each have brought different thoughts with them, each seeks a different way, yet each serves the same source.

One can stand under a great preparation and be in the midst of a hail storm and lose sight of the wanted destination, but one must overcome the outer turmoil of the world. Often lessons of light are painful, but it is the pain as the birth of a child brings pain. Soon the pain is forgotten, forgotten in the joy of that birth, and the goodness that is brought forth from it. There are times of darkness, but there will come light. These things are all needful, but often times one takes upon self that which is not for self. Through your own willingness you can say, "Father, give me this pain, give me the burden and spare the other." That which is to be born can be hidden from others and even from yourself in many ways. It is given only to those who have the eyes to see and the ears to hear that understand the mysteries of God; even as He taught He knew that few understood Him, even as you knowing that there are too few who understand.

There are many worlds as there are many universes. This earth is often referred to as the Red Star, and it too is in the fullness of evolution. Many souls are incarnated in this time who have come voluntarily out of the love in the fullness of their being to guide mankind. There are those that you may meet and pass by without knowing of their missions.They may sit in your very midst and go unrecognized. This is needful, even as you sit in the midst of many and are unrecognized. It is the best way. Your thoughts cannot be given freely, for if they were done in this manner, they would be used adversely by those who seek only to gain the material world. For a man, if he finds a treasure in a field, would go and sell all that he owned that he might buy that field and guard his treasure. These are your treasures. Guard them! and cast ye not your pearls before swine, for these swine would not accept the pearls, but would turn and rend you!

He did not speak idle words, though He spoke in parables. Parables were necessary for all were not ready for His words of light and wisdom. He spoke knowing that there were those who would not contain the words, but would cast them aside for temptation would be too great for them. They whom he chose as His disciples had the preparation and the understanding, though they seemed to be the most ignorant of men. He beheld them not as the world, but as His Brothers, and he entrusted in them secrets of the meanings of His words and charged them with their keeping and sent them forth knowing what the world would do to them. They, in turn, believed in Him, yet knowing what the world would give them in return. They accepted, and they too bore the cross and suffered the death of the world, but attained eternal life.

The simplest of service, though it would seem as nothing of great value can be the difference between the grain of sand and the diamond, and man does not often recognize the diamonds within his life and often puts his values upon the grains of sand. We know that which is within you is good and that which you seek is right. You have the inner knowledge of your convictions then you must stand firmly to that which you hold true and to that which you believe. The world in itself does not have this understanding. It is groping yet in the inner darkness of itself and that is why it is needful for the light that is within you to be released to help eliminate darkness that is in others.

It is in the silence that service manifestations take place, and often times it is in the silence that is your greatest protection. There must be discrimination for the world does not know that which is beyond that vault of silence that cannot be touched, desecrated or crucified. It is a hard lesson to learn. As you are all anxious to share that which you have, and anxious to teach that which you know, but all are not ready to receive that which you have. It is the reason for using discrimination in what you give and to whom you give it. You must see beyond the wall, or as you would say that personality that is shown to you outwardly. Within the depths of their being is their darkness, and within the depths of their being are their pits of hell, even as it is the heights of their heaven, but you see this darkenss and the need of their struggles to be dispelled. It can be done by the right word, the right thought, the right action, the right book, the right prayer, or only in the silence of your love and your light, and this nourishes them even as the sun and the water nourishes the soil, and patience is the time wherein the fruit is brought forth.

Many seek to serve, but demand that it be in their own way, and in so doing they fail to serve their God in His way. Only until they learn that the true service is to serve God according to His will, regardless of the way, regardless of the place, regardless of the person, regardless of the thing involved, and do it in love, in no wise can he serve, and in no wise can he receive until this has been learned. It is a great struggle, but the struggle is beheld, the ultimate goal is known, and we pour our help in love to everyone. Great is our rejoicing at the overcoming. It is with love and compassion that we withhold many things until that one is ready and prepared to receive them. A parent would not give to a child a dangerous thing for the child would be hurt by it, and, until the child becomes an adult would a parent give what he is not prepared to receive and use. Only when the child becomes the adult can he receive it in lieu of them. As you grow and develop, then you become more likened unto the adult, the true God that you are.

SIGNS OF THE TIME

BEHOLD ALL MANNERS OF THINGS shall come to pass, and these shall be the signs, the signs of the time, for time shall be, and there shall be times and times again, and time. There will be much, but behold within the elements of nature, and then within the elements of human nature, and it is accomplished. Yes! there are many voices lifted even now in prophecy of this time and many are aware and many cry out and say, Behold! Listen! Know!, and yet though the ears of man hear, yet they hear not; though they listen but contain not once the speaker ceases speaking, the hearer goes forth and returns as he came. I would say to you many are the voices of spirit, many are the workers within the vineyard, but many are even as the sower of the seeds in fertile ground. You have seeded well, and soon will this seed come forth, and it shall be harvested in joy, for the fruit it will bear shall be good.

SOUL

I SPEAK TO YOU BELOVEDS, for beloved you are indeed. For greater love is there not than this that you have of spirit, and greater love is there not than that of our Father for his precious ones, for no matter how much man attains in the world and in worldly things and attain not his soul, he hath nothing and is lost. I say unto you dearly beloved greater are thy attainments of the spirit and greater is the love of the Father for His children. Blessed art thou, and yea blessed shalt thou be! You shall behold the secrets that are hidden from the hearts and minds of others, and they shall be revealed unto you in a most hidden place of the deep and their secrets shall you know. How many struggle to wrest these secrets! Yet the Father can give only to those to whom he loves dearly revealing unto them vast treasures, treasures which are yours. They are not for the naked eye, but they are a part of the soul, and I would say unto you, "Blessed art thou," and listen and know that all is secure, all is yours and all is well!

I would speak these words to you, for I have walked this valley of tears, I have passed through the vale, and I have walked alone many times and know well the contentions, know well the contritions and the tears of our sins; therefore, I say hearken to this that I give unto you, the most precious of things—the love of God, a joyous spirit, and the blessing and protection of the love of God you would see is yours.

SPECIAL DAYS

FOR THIS DAY that has been set aside to do the work and the will of God is a day to send forth of your own light and your own love. It is a giving freely into the hands of the spirit to accomplish all things to the glory of God. It is the appointing to their use your light and your love. It is the dedication of your being as their instruments. It is the contemplation that you have made within your temples. It is the sanctification of the spirit, and, coming together in this time, behold only the light of God that never fails and pour it unstintingly unto all.

Even as it is written for your understanding the sun shines upon the just and the unjust, and the rain falls upon the just and the unjust, and it is given freely and equally to all. But they who are receptive and serve God receive the true abundance of all things spiritual, and, they who do not, yet also partake of the sun and rain and know not these things nor are they rewarded by them. Nonetheless the sun and rain provides the help, sustains the life and blesses all. So must your life go forth, and it must go forth freely to bless all, the just as well as the unjust.

No man knoweth when his Lord cometh and no man, until he stands beside the Father, knows the full extent of the use of his light. Even in places hidden from man's mind and knowledge, this light goes forth and it is used and is accomplished. It is as even as the words spoken milleniums ago that have brought forth much good and much light in the minds of man in this day, even as your light is sent forth does it accomplish, and is a far reaching thing, for it is a power that is eternal and flows infinitely.

Perhaps in these few words you may perceive the idea and understanding of eternity, and, being eternal, it is only to they who sustain within themselves the light and the truth that are thus molded, trained and taught the uses of the light. It is a power that cannot be unleashed to all men and can be given only into the hands of those found most worthy and even then it is not a thing lightly given.

Wherein the reward? The reward is found within the worthiness to serve God. You have been told, man seeks the reward in all that he does in the day of his doing, but he who seeks to serve God shall receive his reward in his time. In giving good freely must it be done with no thought of return. Herein lies true love, true charity, but to do unto others in the demand that it is returned by them is at a loss. How many times has man said and repeated the words, "Do ye unto others that which you would have them do unto you?" but he has misconstrued the true meaning, for in this wise if a man be good unto his fellowman and be sincere and free in his goodness, then will this goodness return unto him a thousand fold. Should he seek his reward in the days of his giving, he shall find it not, for those who are of the world their reward is with them.

I say to you, which is the greater to smile when there is naught to smile for, or to weep when there is naught but weeping? Send forth your light, behold not the iniquity, but see the light as accomplishing and being as good. Weep not over the evils of man, but rejoice in your own overcoming. The ways of the world are with them, but the ways of God are with you.

It is good for you to speak of these things with one another and to weigh them carefully, but I say unto you cast aside that which is not worthy of you. Often in the expression of bringing thoughts and words into the open in conversaion releases them from within, but then dismiss that which is not worthy of you and it becomes as nothing.

I behold the fountain of light. I behold it pouring forth and behold it as a blessing and a rejoicing in it. You have been told this is not for the weak, but for the strong in spirit.

You have not been promised the easiest of ways, but neither have you gone without the comfort and the help. You have gained by your merits alone, and it is by the merit of the soul that these things are of a reward unto you. You will find, as you have in the past, that which you learn and gain is sweeter through the gaining of your own self. You know that which you have learned and retained through experience. You have gathered and gained knowledge and you have retained and grown.

SPIRIT

WHAT A GREAT THING you have been given! I repeat, a bed of thorns, but not without roses; valleys, but not without the hills; darkness but not without light; trials but not without the help; tribulations but not without the comfort; agonies, but not without the understanding. No, not one thing without the compassion of spirit; not one thing without the understanding of the love; not one thing, for within the spirit is no lack. You see lack. There is no lack in God or spirit. There is no lack in love. Lack is only in man, but when man seeks spirit and the love of God he lacks nothing. The world heaps upon that one the lack they find within their own selves, beholding not the completeness and the wholeness of that individual who has found God and spirit, and is love because of these things. I say unto you the lack is within others, for they behold not, nor see it, for they look and judge another by the lack within their own beings.

As you set aside a time to do the work and the will of God make it a day to send forth your own light and your own love as well. It is a giving freely into the hands of the spirit to accomplish all things to the glory of God. It is the appointing to spirit's use your light and your love. It is the dedication of your being their instrument. It is the contemplation that you have made within your temple. It is the sanctification of the spirit, and coming together in a time to behold only the light of God that never fails and pour it unstintingly unto all.

They who come unto us seeking for truth, for light and for love in its divinity, seek out the higher octaves of light. Only as the spirit of each one is prepared is the ability to reach the higher places and to receive therefrom. These things must be sought earnestly and with a sincere heart and desire for them. It is in the seeking that is the growing, the developing and the strengthing. You have been told this is not for the weak, but for the strong in spirit. You have not been promised the easiest of ways, but neither have you gone without the comfort and the help. You will find as you have in the past, that which you learn and gain is sweeter through the gaining of your ownself. You know that which you have learned and retained through experience. You will see what you have gathered and what knowledge you have gained and have retained and thereby grown.

The things of the spirit are simple things to learn and understand. They who seek to dwell in the spirit, to work in the spirit, and to express the spirit, contend more with the world. Though you live in this world and are not a part of it, you become seemingly more a part than others. You deal with life strongly and life is washed upon your doorstep to be dealt with by you.

This one has sought understanding of all things, seeking spirit first and understanding of man last. Many are put in this way for an understanding, but are so guided by spirit in giving understanding to this one realize not the part they play, nor the role they have been called upon to play, and being impressed, they give much of their own personal ego. You have been told to be of a discerning mind, weigh that which you receive, sort the grains from the chaff, seek truth; thereby, receiving truth and know that which is beheld within you is most worthy and that which you have attained through the overcoming, not only of self or personality, but overcoming also that which is within others. We have tried to explain that each individual must learn, overcome and attain through their own beings. That which is given by words, understanding, love, example and steadfastness in faith is the greatest help given to mankind.

Man aspires to the wisdom of the ancients and the knowledge that was given, yet in doing so there lurks within the self the secret greed of mankind. Knowing these things they, therefore, are given only to those who are prepared to receive them, only to those whom they know will use them with spiritual value, only to those that they know will bring forth divine will to glorify God—not self or spirit, for spirit seeks not the glory for itself, but seeks to glorify the Infinite Father in all things.

That which takes place at this time, dark as though it may seem as an evil to mankind, it is these same people that will be helped most by it, for that which they commit to bring unhappiness, anguish, and sorrow within your lives will one day return and shall be a help. Yes, even as a help unto them in overcoming their own selves, for many times man learns only through the anguish of the realization of what he has committed, not only against himself, but against his brethren.

It is well to seek understanding of all things, but to seek spirit first is the better thing, rather than to seek the understanding of man first. Many are put in this way for an understanding, but are so guided by spirit in giving understanding of this.

The things of spirit may be of many natures, in many different ways, and be of many things, but each thing is a part of the whole, though man beholds it not, and cannot see how one thing fits into place with another.

STRENGTH OF THE SOUL

I HAVE HEARD within the echoes of your heart the words of "Thank you Father," and I bathe in the peace and quiet that pervades now this temple, and I partake of the sweetness of the joy that shall soon fill it, for in the anticipation of good, good comes, and in the sincere prayer of love, love is; and in the trust and belief of hope is fulfillment.

I commend you for you have come a long arduous way and the strings that thou hast severed from your heart have been painful, but they have accomplished the good and once the releasement of these things has taken place, then is the freedom for the fulfillment within you. I have found within my brothers the hardest task to accomplish is to release all things and to reevaluate their values, but once this is accomplished then all things work toward good, for each must accomplish within the self and in the accomplishment of the self is the joy and rejoicing in the accomplishments of others. You have been told to know Christ and to understand "The Christ," one must be a Christ.

As you know the strength of the soul is founded in weaknesses and the growth is through struggles. You know the terror and pain of the darkness are great and the overcoming into the light is sweet and most wonderful. It is a peace that man cannot tell of in words alone. It is the inner sanctuary wherein God sits and man cannot enter nor desecrate, and though the world about you is in chaos and seemingly falling into pieces, the calm within you cannot be touched. The peace and the knowledge of your Father within you is your salvation and is your greatest accomplishment. In gaining this thing, I say unto you, beloved sisters, the security, the knowledge, the light and above all the love that pours forth from you expands your peace to others, and they look to you for their strength.

In becoming this fountain of light love is the healing, is the strength, is the blessing that flows forth. The blessing is not controlled by man, but given freely by God. There is no stopping of this power, for once it is released it cannot be withheld. No. Not even you, though I know full well that the thought of it would not enter into your mind. The inner quality is the magnetism of love, of faith, the strength of the soul that draw all others, for even as He, the Blessed One, who said "I go," but I draw all men unto me.

SYMBOLS

THERE ARE MANY SYMBOLS, but the symbols are empty. Yes, man makes symbols, but these are empty and only when he comes to know that they are only symbols and finds God within himself will he fully realize the gift. There is no greater thing and I give mine.

TEMPLE OF LEARNING

I HAVE COME TO SPEAK with you this morning—to counsel you to enter the temple of learning often. Its doors are accessible to you, you but have to desire to enter therein. You seek to broaden your mind, then know that you may enter into this temple of learning at all times and time again. You seek to develop yourself spiritually, know you then that the fires are not merciful. They are all consuming and self is the first to be consumed. To become spiritually illumined, you must seek to become like he who came to show you the way. You must find the strength within yourself to overcome.

There are times that words used are very stern, as a parent would chastise a child. The chastisement is for the child's good. You love your children and would not give them that which was not good for them. How much greater is the love of your Father for you. If man is evil he gives good to his child, then God being good gives so much more to his children? He is a just God. God is not mocked, for nothing is hid from Him and He said often "vengeance is mine." Believe you this thing?

I taught my pupils to stand but with love. I taught them saying: "Man know thyself, be true to thy ownself and seek ye ever truth." I taught them abstract thinking—the mind to question and seek the answers to those questions, not to be ruled over by another man's mind in fear or in jealousy, or in slavery. Each man is free, each man is an individual. Each man should seek to rule only himself, and not others. If man learns to live in this wise, therein lies his paradise. Truth is bitter, but it is as good meat. It is a hard master, but a worthy one. It is as elusive as the light of day—the dark of night, and it is as only man is ready to receive it. What is true today may no longer be true tomorrow. Man grows, develops and expands, and truth can come to him only in the fullness of that growth. What is true to one may not hold for another. I charge you seek ever truth, for it is the essence of life.

Come ye into the inner temple to receive thy truths and thy learnings, take off thy sandals and shake the dust from thy feet, cast off thy outer garments, for only they who wear robes of the spiritual enter into this Holy Place.

THANKFULNESS OF SPIRIT

THANK YOU! THANK YOU! I thank you for the moments of your time given. I thank you for the light and love. I thank you for the prayers said for others. I thank you for the call for help. I thank you for your needs that I may be of service. I thank you for all the loveliness within you. I thank you for the beauty of your thought. I thank you for the love within you're feeling. I thank you for the strength in your faith. I thank you for these things are needful by us. I thank you for the hands freely given. I thank you for that which is daily given up at the alter of the Creator. I thank you! I bless you! I love you!

THOUGHT

MY EYES BEHOLD THE WORLD and her many wounds. There are those who come forth to gather the grapes from the vineyards and those who would bind the wounds. These are the signs of the time. Behold with the eyes of your soul and rise above the thoughts of man. Become not enmeshed with the thought realms of man. It would bind you to a lower level. Free yourselves! Broaden the horizons of your vision! Learn to behold the fullness of the pattern—not one small portion! Often man becomes so engrossed in the small portion of a pattern, he is blind to the whole of it.

It is even as your own lives. You become so enmeshed in your problems, you cannot see beyond. You must learn to withdraw from your problems that binds you close and see them at a distance, in order to get the true vision. It is even as the artist paints his canvas. It is from the distance the true vision of the painting is beheld, for at close hand, often times, the colors and forms are blurred and seem to run into one another, but at a distance all these things focus and become clear. So it is with lessons of truth. Man is not able yet to receive them, for his vision is blurred, and it is necessary to teach him in parables for his understanding. Clear your vision that you may receive the truth without parables. Truth is often an instant of recognition within your own being, and in that instant a thousand words are understood. The mind suddenly comprehends and is no longer the same, for it has grown and it has expanded.

Man does not realize that which he does in ignorance, for if he could behold it, he would do so in terror, for every thought is either constructive or destructive, and a destructive thought is as powerful as the constructive one. In man's thinking he must learn to build constructive thought, for it too carries momentum. When thou looketh upon aught that is life, see the perfection that is in it, for you not only bless that life, but in turn are blessed by it. Thought is a most powerful weapon and it must be used for good.

Thought is power. It is the most powerful feeling. It is the next powerful, and thought and feeling combined are a power that man does not know the full extent of, for as he thinks, so he is. As he aspires, so he can become. As his feelings are, they rule his physical system. Where there dwells harmony and love, therein is peace and strength, therein is a system in good order.

Man has said space is empty, a vacuum, but it is not, and I say to you there is no vacuum that all is living thought. All is harmony and balance and could not be otherwise, for it was created from the perfect source, which is harmony and peace and balance, which is purity, which is love, and which is light. In the order of the systems, these things must be, for there is but one system. There are many. This is but one part of the whole, one part of the galaxies. Beyond are many worlds.

See your own being as a fountain of light. It is pure. Under your own conscious direction send that light forth and see it touch all that you love and know. Use it to flood as a mighty water that in which you work. Then extend it forth that it may bless all who serve the light that it may cleanse and purify your home land, and from this point send it forth to every nation. Perceive it as it pushes back the darkness. Perceive it as it annihilates all that is less than itself, and know that it is a living and intelligent thing you deal with, for it is thought, and thought is the basis of all things. In the beginning was the word and the word was with God and God was the word, and the word was formed from the thought. Thought is the whole picture. The word puts it forth into its creation, and know that the word is "I AM." This is the word, the key. This is your all, in all, eternally sustained.

Over the years, centuries and eons, man has sought the light, for within him is the truth, and the truth that is within him shall seek its own. You have read and you have been told truth. Light and love are the things the Blessed One came to teach. It is He who said, "I am the door, I am the way, and man who seeks me is one with me, and one with me is one with the Father." Then truly he may stand and say, even as I, "I and the Father are one, and he who believes in this, greater things shall he do than I have done." Think well for this is a state of being, and this is a state of thinking and knowing. It is in the knowing and the becoming that greater things than these ye shall do also. Conceive the fullness of that promise. Behold! the magnitude of those words. Herein lies your wisdom, herein lies your fulfillment. It is accomplished in the knowing, and it is truth. Seek ye ever truth and follow ye ever the light, for it is life. Even as truth was given in that Blessed Book in the form of parables, man could not receive truth in its fullness and even as He, our Beloved, said to thee, "There are many things that I would tell you, but you are not ready to receive them." You are now ready to receive, and you, in the days to come much shall be unfolded to you for your understanding.

You have been told God's thoughts are not your thoughts, or you would be God, and not man as you are. God's ways are not man's ways and he chooses the simple and the ignorant, the pure of heart, and the pure of mind with which to work through, to express his divinity, his wisdom, his will, his love and his way. It is the learned and the wise men of the world that behold not the wisdom of God, for they would twist it and would turn it and force it into the slots of their own thinking that it should conform. This cannot be done nor ever will it be. The simple shall continue to confound the wise, and the wise will learn from the simple and find within themselves that they have only the wisdom that the world can give. The wisdom of God is immortal, the wisdom of man is as a thing that passes in the night, and returneth not, nor endureth, but the Word of God endureth, for it is eternal.

TIME

TIME IS AN ELEMENT that man weighs, values, prices, and works feverishly within, but I say again time is of essence and time is eternity. That time which is spent in this perfection and overcoming is valued far more than any gain or renown of worldly things. Is it not better to be a perfect instrument in the hands of God for no matter how short a time, as man measures it, than a poor instrument in the time of measurement of man for God's work? I say unto you once more, time is of an essence to spirit and is valued in growth of the soul, for time is eternity as well as reality, and when man comprehends and applies time, he will use it more wisely. He will gain greatly from every moment allotted to him in the physical form he now occupies.

That which mankind has taken centuries to build and become can be spanned within one life time with the use of his time rightly. I speak on this discourse of time as a thing of the mind and its uses. There is not one second of your time, as you measure it, without its blessing, without its gain, without its measure of value. No matter how small and little a day's time may seem in your life, it has its gain, its blessings, and its learnings. You must learn to find beauty and joy even in the skill of the working hand, as well as the beauty of the word and of the eye. If you can for a few moments contemplate on God, your Father, on His beauty, His truth, His perfection, His goodness, you will gain much.

Yes, I have been asked to talk to you of the past of your time, and I want to clarify time as to the past. There is only the present, and as the Beloved said, "Live ye now in the nowness of time, for this is your time. It is now." I would say to you that which the world honors is light, and had its beginning in lands which man today knows; leaders in teaching of this in their time, were not known. In their time only they who had the illumination, the understanding appreciated and knew that which was theirs, but all mankind did not know. Only after a lapse of a period of time has man recognized the light. It hasn't always been recognized. It always was and always will be. Nothing is lost. This is light.

Behold the light of the world is to come and man in his mind cannot possibly visualize the conception of the spirit, for he seeks only the conceptions of the physical. Man, who has achieved a level of illumination is not satisfied within his own being at the level that he has been illuminated, for if he should, he would not progress. He seeks ever to learn, he seeks further illumination, and he shall receive it in abundance, but he knowth not when his Lord cometh with his gift.

There are many things to be said in a short time, and I will waste as little time—as you term time wasted, for we see time as an element that is unending and eternal. You see time as limited and feel the need and pressure of accomplishment in a short space. Now I would say unto you to hold the thought of eternity in all things, for then you release this time element into the hands of the power from which you seek help. In dealing with these things, look deep into the heart of your own self and behold it is as already done, for it has been said unto you, according to your faith shall it be done unto you. Greater faith hath no man than this that he found in the one who came unto Him and said, "Master, say that it is done, and I know that it is done," and he went away rejoicing in his heart saying, "He hath said and I know." Recall this parable? Good, for in it lies a key for you also, and it is a key for all and the time shall come when you will give many keys to many people.

Now indeed there is a season for all things and a time for resting, a time for accomplishment and a time for standing back. Behold in the days to come you shall see a time for standing back. This is good in many ways, not only for you, but for others who have the need of the awareness of the accomplishments you have brought forth. It is only through this awareness that they themselves will see wherein they have lacked, and, in this measure, perhaps overcome many things that have been needful of overcoming.

I speak of the element of time, for in man's thinking time must be recorded according to moments, years, seconds, days, weeks, months, centuries, eons, but again I say "time is eternal." It is in the nowness—always in the nowness. That which you accomplish in the flowing of time is past, only the accomplishment remains. Always live in the nowness, but retain the accomplishment. The mind of man has the facility of memory and herein records incidents whether aware or unaware of the incident occuring.

The recording of time is much like this machine you use (tape recorder) for it records every incident of moment of breath. Now I will endeavor to elaborate on this subject. I speak of the moment of breath. It is the moment of stepping from life into life. Man does not die, nor has man ever been dead. It is a flowing of light into the instruments or channel of expression. When that instrument or channel has completed the purpose, the accomplishment, it then goes on. There is deterioration only in the use of the vessel when it is no longer of use. From the moment of breath man records the span that he has been given. In the facility of memory can he record incidents, even to accomplish the purpose of learning, for only when man learns has he accomplished. There are errors, but errors with purpose. (question) Does error have a purpose? (answer) Yes, but man cannot see purpose in error.

I speak to you of this for many shall be confronted with error and contend with error, but man in his mindness of self sees not beyond the error and many times in answer it is withheld. It is through the struggle of man to find that answer withheld, that the greater accomplishment can be done. Soon you will see in retrospective manner how the many events of life in their entanglements have been woven for a purpose and in retrospect, in being objective, you will find the understanding. It is only when man induces the personal emotion that the object is then learned, but not seen clearly. Once the overcoming of the emotional aspect has begun would there seem to be a lack? Again I say there is no lack.

Soon this seeming lack of emotion transforms into divine indifference, and gives freely of its love and compassion, for it has attained its accomplishment. It is no longer personally touched and is not emotionally involved. This is not a lack. It is an attainment and a necessary attainment for these days to come. Many situations will demand your complete control, your complete self-mastery, and in all seeking the mastery of self is most important. It is the control of the mental, the emotional and their effects upon the physical. Once on this path the barrier becomes greater, and the obstacles more difficult, the way more dark, but I say unto you again it is in the will to struggle, to overcome and to become. It is then you are rewarded greatly, for indeed then you become one and are able to speak always with authority.

On the quest of the ultimate, the closer to the goal of the ultimate the more difficult it becomes. It is only in your preparation to have the strength to see the ultimate, for it is your purpose to function with the ultimate. You see not beyond the vast purpose of your being, or have you beheld the all-over pattern that you have touched, for within your years more accomplishment of the spirit has been done than the mind can grasp. The vastness of this will one day be revealed to your knowledge; still you grope within your spirit for you see not. I would say behold through the eyes of humility and through this will you see, for that which we behold is indeed a great thing.

TOLERANCE

THE GREATEST THING AND NEED in man is tolerance, tolerance of humanity in the knowledge that in humanity lies the seeds of the soul and that every being has to progress through humanity to acquire his spiritual state of being. This is a necessary thing, and life in this classroom, or the schoolroom of the universe, which we call the earth planet, is a desired thing and is a privileged thing. Slowly as man would look upon its history as it has evolved, this too is a natural and necessary thing.

Always in each century are those beings who have developed spiritually and who have become a light for all men, not only for his century, but the centures yet to be, for the Infinite provides all things in perfection of order. Each one precious, each life necessary, in each moment something to learn and absorb, for man may live one life, or he may live a hundred lives in one span of life. The span of years may be short or may be long to his term of counting life.

Count not the years you seek to have, but accept the days which the Infinite One has blessed you with. Work therein toward its fulfillment and in the course of its time all is taken care of. They who fail to do this thing, others are provided to take up their place and accomplish it. Yes, this was given unto you as an understanding of why many things are not completed that would seemingly be necessary to be completed by one person in one life time.

Yes, everyone who has something to give unto mankind is what you have been told, have many times considered, and have looked upon as being peculiar or different, are indeed these things. In the knowledge of being these things in the eyes of the world is the soul satisfaction of knowing, but it is the Infinite that judges, excutes and fulfills.

TRUST

I SEE MANY CLOUDS, but I also see much light, I could say unto you in your coming, in your preparation, use light, but know light also. Even as now I show you lights as a flame that grows and in growing is encompassing all things and meets in that union with your light also. Yes, things of the world grow heavy, but only when the mind takes much thought of these things. I tell you again, as once before, take even all things you call of the world as the yarn in a tangled state of being and place them in hands of spirit and leave them. Human thought taking and worry make knots in the threads and makes it more difficult to unwind the tangles to be a smooth skein.

Be as little child and bring things to spirit and leave things with spirit, for as a child leave things to parent or friend, he goes off happy knowing that love of this one makes all things all right. Learn! Trust Spirit! All things will be made right.

Even in these days, there is much struggling, but even in these days is there much light. These are necessary things at times to test your strength and your trust.

It is often as you trust. You put the cake in the oven and test it to see if it is done. If it is not done, you put it back in the oven to finish baking, but you carefully watch that the fire does not burn the cake; only that it be baked long enough and is good. You feed many people and you put much love in things you make and you find joy in your heart at their pleasure of eating these things you make. Even so with spirit that makes many things and gives many things and takes great pleasure and joy in your joy and pleasure of these things of spirit.

I speak from the heart of one who has seen much in the world. I speak with compassion given through their own trials and sorrow and through my own joy and through my own happiness of heart. I see many changes in world of man, but man does not see change. Yes! Yes! speaking I was called Grandmother by many, many. I was called wise woman by my people, but wisdom came only from spirit working in me. From life I took many things for my wisdom to know and to understand my people.

There are greater things than fear. To overcome fear, to gain courage, and in gaining it will be the overcoming of other things. Fear is to be feared only for fear itself.

TRUTH

WE WILL DEAL WITH TRUTH FIRST. You have no doubt found that truth is relative to the understanding you have gained in thinking of God's law. He would tell you, "Truth is One, changeless, eternal." Man divorces himself from truth, for he finds the darkness more to his liking. He fears not the darkness. He fears the light, and yet the light is his salvation and his life. Good is found in all men, for man is created in the image of God, but even the good within all men is misused by man. Inherently is he, his Father, and inherently will he also be as his Father. They who would seem to stagnate within the realms of the spiritual and of the mind withhold their own progression and contend against those who progress. Yet all are of one spirit, but are not all of one understanding. In "the time," they too will progress and reach the understanding, for no man can exist or be in existence except by the Father, and we speak of the "Eternal Father."

Truth is a simple thing, but man makes it a complexity of things. He recognizes the truth, but refuses to accept it as truth in this wise. It has taken centuries for man to evolve, and we but wait for completion of man's evolution.

Truth cannot be proven to man. Man must prove truth to his own self. There can be much understanding of spirit, but if there be no firmness or control of the self he cannot come to the understanding of self. Humility must be learned if self is overcome. The things of the spirit must be dealt with in the strength of the spirit, not weakness of self. I speak in the wise of the ego. In teaching truth the ears are deaf because the ego thinks it does not apply to them.

There are so many who cry out in prayer and supplication; if only they would know that the answer is waiting and would hold fast, for often in the waiting is the greatest test of the human. In holding fast, it is the accomplishment. It is the fulfillment of the desire and it is the answer. Only truth, only light, and only love, can be the command to the highest to bring forth that which is of the highest. In all the commanding, command you truth, for truth is being, truth is one, truth is all.

Truth is one, and they who seek truth and seek it with a single purpose and a oneness of thought and being opens the way more fully for truth to be given. Truth in its purity cannot be received by all men, for all men understand it not. Therefore, it has been found necessary to reach man through many instruments according to the level of his understanding. Many must be taught in parable form as a child would be taught. Many receive truth in its pure form through the thought and feeling world of their own being. They who seek in the lower forms of truth are seeking truth nonetheless and they need guidance. From that level they seek to the higher levels, the road has many perils and can be most danerous. To become enmeshed only in the psychic plane is to become lost in many ways. Each must rise above this plane, and it is in the higher planes of spiritual truth that man must seek and obtain. There are those who will come into this place seeking only the psychic. Guide them that they may seek beyond, that they may lift the thoughts of their mind to that which is beyond.

Man obscures truth in its purity and would apply his own meanings that they be more acceptable to himself. These things must pass away, and I speak of the things of man. Truth must be given in its purity and fullness, whether it be acceptable to man or not, for all things of man shall pass away but truth shall never pass away. He who came to be witness of the truth shall give the truth, and it shall be the light unto the world and a lamp unto man's feet.

Stand for that which is truth, waiver not to the right nor to the left. Man would adulterate truth. You must hold truth unadulterated. There are many who come to speak His word and give of their own understanding, but I say unto he who hath understanding of Me, understandeth all things that are of Me, and need not another man's interpretation and understanding.

Truth is one. It is a whole piece, even as you work you see only the part you are accomplishing, yet you know it will be complete in its eventuality. See even now the pattern is unfolding, and behold your part in the weaving. It is a thing of great beauty. Many are his instruments. Blessed are they. Spirit in it highest form of evolution is pure, and the pure of heart see God, and behold Him within them, and rejoice, for they realize that they have life eternal, even as you have been given eternal waters of life. I behold your joy, for man must lose first before he regains and holds, and that which you think is lost is but yours more abundantly, for it is in the losing that it is found.

I behold the light that dwells within this room, and I behold the light that dwells within you. I behold many changes, and I behold a great overcoming. You have done well. It is necessary often, for in bringing forth truth and lessons of truth and light, that there be the open mind and the open heart. It is needful for the soul that seeks to accept fully and to counter it not. Truth is a complexity of things to man, but it is simplicity to us, for even as beauty is exacting, it is pure, and it is simple, for it is perfection, and how often you have heard, "Become ye perfect, even as your Father is in Heaven is perfect." It is the perfection of self. It is becoming one with the Father, the overself, the oversoul, or as it is called the "I Am." It is becoming and perfecting the outer in complete harmony with the inner. It is a great task.

You have progressed and the greatest progress made is through the help and compassion of others, for as you seek to help another, you help yourself. The compassion and love that is given in spirit are received ten fold over unto thine ownself. It is the maxim, in order to receive, first you must give, for it is in the giving that you receive most abundantly. This is not understood in its real sense, for it is a thing of the soul, of the spirit.

Often man thinks I will give one pair of shoes today that I may receive two pairs tomorrow. It is not in this wise that he shall receive, but most likely he will lose two pairs of shoes on the morrow. Giving must be done freely, from the love of the heart, and it must be done of the innermost being, and yet it must be done in wisdom, and it must be done without thought of self, and it is in this wise that it is received.

Seek always for the pure state of being in these things and in all things that are given unto you, for man must search for truth and be of a discerning mind in the truth that he seeks, whether or not he accepts it as being, or in his transient state, or in its purity. He has blessed you with this light.

UNFOLDMENT

THE LOVE IN MY HEART greets the love in yours. The light of my soul drinks the light of yours, and my footsteps will be your footsteps, for I come to give you love and to add to the courage within you and to bless the faith.

I see this time has been well prepared for. I see an unfoldment in you much better, much greater. If man could see the unfoldment of himself as spirit sees, how great would be his joy and how much more would he struggle in his unfoldment. I say it is as a blind man who cannot see, yet feels about him the world in which he dwells. When he stumbles and hands reach out to help him, and when he cries out for help, there are many who come to help him and there are many who hear his cries and comes to help him. Then he knows the world he lives in and is no more blind.

Man who seeks understanding of spirit is like one blinded, but spirit is there, but not seeing spirit, often rejects spirit as not being. Many know and cry out for help and cry to see, and in their journey they receive the sight and behold that which they dwell within, and those who came to them. Great is his rejoicing, even as the blind man who cried out, "whereas before I did not see, now I see; whereas before I was blind, I am no longer blind, and I behold the face of my Lord." Great was his rejoicing in these things.

Even as the Great Brother spoke saying there be two men who owed much money, one man paid all he owed, the other man could not pay, and when called upon to pay he to whom the money was owed forgave him and great was his rejoicing. The man who paid all the money said, "Lord why forgive this one what he owed, and I who owed paid all received not such rejoicing." His Lord said to him, "He who rejoices more, it is he who is forgiven more, and it is he who loveth more." This is for you to think upon and to know that he who has sinned more than his brother has been forgiven more, and he would rejoice and love more, so I say he who struggles most in spirit great is his joy in receiving spirit, but he to whom all things are given in an easy way know not the joy and the love in his heart.

Now I would say one other thing to you, and I speak in words of my Brother. He who believes and has faith in that which he asks of his Father shall receive it, but he who believes not in what he asks receives not, so in asking believe you receive and it is yours.

VIBRATION

WORD IS SOUND, and in speaking, sound is vibration. Each spirit has its own ray. In speaking of that ray of vibration is your contact with spirit. Even the name of each one is a ray of vibration, even as your name, and they who speak your name touch you through its rate of vibration. When you speak the name of any one of your teachers that one touches you, for you have touched their vibration of their name in the speaking. I have been brought in contact with you, so the giving of my name, and in giving of your light, you in turn receive my blessing.

THE WAYS OF GOD

MAN KNOWS NOT, nor understands the ways of God. The ways may seem foolish, but to look deep and to understand his ways are wise, and only foolish in the eyes of the world. In this is wisdom, for man struggles not, nor does he contend against the foolish things, but he will tolerate them and even accept them. He fears not what he thinks is foolish, but they who accept the ways of God are wise and are blessed by them. Such love! It is there! It is intangible, and yet it is tangible. It is unseen, but it is felt. It is yet unknown in its fullness. God is love, and it is with this love that we enfold you.

WELCOME

WELCOME! Welcome to the inner circle of light. Welcome into the ethers of the abstract thought. Welcome into the regions of the soul. Come and walk the paths of truth and walk the paths of light, for only when one turns from darkness to paths of light does he find the way. Come! cast aside the ferrets! cast aside the chains! cast away all limitations and come!

Before you now unfolds the vastness of the horizons, the Infinite of Eternity, the whole of the spirit wherein all is and ever shall be. Come! Lift! Lift! the heart, the mind, the spirit. Let these things soar even as the eagle soars above the mountain tops. Cast out all weakness that you may be strong. Within you has not that been built? Has it not been found worthy? Have not you the faith of the master builder? Know you not that which has been built is good and that all is well? To count this thing as being otherwise is to be in doubt of the craft of the Master.

Only as the pits of weaknesses and of doubts are cast aside and replaced with the faith that faileth not, are these things that test the ability and the strength. Therefore, I bid thee come, come into the sanctuaries, come into the coolness and the quietness of the inner self wherein lies all the beauty, all truth, all peace within the regions of worlds that man has yet to seek and find. Herein lies all that you would seek to know or have. Such a simple thing and yet complicated only in the ability to release.

It is not only a welcoming, but it is a pleasure for us to be with you. Yes, even greater than the pleasure you anticipate and feel in being with us. You wonder how this is possible that spirit can rejoice greater at a union than you do, but the human knows its joy of the human experiences; therefore, when I welcome you, I welcome you with great joy.

WILL

IN ALL THY SEEKINGS, seek love, and in all things truth and understanding. Man fails to realize that truth and love overshadows all things. Is is not only the expansion of the heart, but also the expansion of the mind. It is the purity of the heart, the simplicity of the soul. These are the greatest treasures of man; then all men are free to possess them, but man confuses these things in the course of his life, for man imposes his own will and thinking on his brother and desires to dictate a way of life. Christ did not dictate, but gave freely through the example of his own life, a way of living for man.

It is strange that the world clouds the sight in man's reasoning, for man has come to live by the ways of the world and not the ways of spirit. Even those who follow the light and seek to become one with it, often lets the world obscure their thinking and seeing with the eye of their own spirit.

Man in his intrigues of the mind brings about the upheavals around him, for it is thought carried into action. It too has its power, even as the thought of light carried into action has its power also. Therefore, I charge you to bring divine thought into action with the use of the light. Command it be sent forth! See it within the self as covering the multitudes going forth into the very bowels of the earth, and then poured forth out into the universe itself! See within you the etheric belts around this earth planet in lavender, in blue and then in white!

You have within you the power of the use of this light. Use it, and use it well. Let no negativity of thought enter at any time. I repeat, "no negativity" of thought, for this cancels out that which you have sent in positive thinking. Once you have learned that in this work only the thought of its perfection and completion should be held inviolate and doubted at no time that no negative thought enter. It is only then can the fulfillment come forth unscarred. Contemplate these words! Think about them! Know them within your being, for within you must be that place untouched, unscarred, and unviolated! Within you, you must build this Holy Place, and let no doubt or negativity wound and scar it. If you do allow doubt and negativity it is then that you, yourself, allow these things to be still born. You, yourself, cancel out that which you would bring forth into glory.

YOUR MISSION

DO NOT CONTEND with the thought that you feel you have not given unto others adequately or fully, for you have given unto others. It is their choice to take that which you have given unto them, and put it into use and apply it to themselves. This choice is theirs. Man cannot change man. Do you not see about you that which is called charity, that which would change the environment of man hasn't occurred to that man, not until the choice of the individual can that individual be changed, or bettered, or lifted. So that you do not misunderstand it, I say to you it is necessary for all the nations, all the light bearers to realize that which they give is like a spark that can ignite within the breast of another the slumbering coals that they burst into flame. The warm seeds may fall on unknown grounds and grow in abundance, and when you know not, your harvest comes in full to overflowing. Nothing loses by chance. Spirit strengthens. The contentions of life are mostly on this plane. One must deal with individuals composingly or comparatively, and stand firm for what they are and for what they have become. Your light should so shine forth that the one unkown to you would see it and become that light too.

Is this not your mission to give unto mankind the light, the knowledge, the spiritual? I speak strongly to bring forth your inner convictions and speak out of love and compassion, for I see the falterings and the weaknesses in the feelings of not knowing the accomplishment, but I say to you in the light all things are known.

YOUR PLACE

WHEN GOD HAS CALLED his own and said, "Come from without and leave all and follow me," it is the leaving of the ways of the world, the world's thinking, the world's judging and the world's being and taking upon you the ways of the spirit, the thinking of the spirit, and the being of the spirit. This is not a simple thing, but it is most rewarding for wherein this thing *is*, you can glorify the Father. Think upon these things within your mind and heart and know you are to live within this world, yet contend not with it, nor be a part of it. In so doing you are seeming to be more a part of the world and seeming to live more fully in it than ever. The greater the contention against the heart, the stronger the spirit becomes, for the stronger the fire burns, the swifter is the purifying and the cleaning. Think not, for in all things know that we are ever with you, no matter how dark. There is always the light.

I see the thoughts that tumble one onto the other and reach forth into the future and are diverse in many ways, for the thoughts of the heart reach out to many places in seeking to understand many things, and human nature is the most difficult. Each thing will fall into place, even as the mason that builds the house, first the foundation must be laid and each stone put into place, so that it is well built. If he should rush and hurry and does not this work well, then the foundation is not well built and would crumble and not withstand the storms. Each thing that enters within you, deal with it one at a time. Each thing will fall into its proper place and when you view the handiwork of your own being it shall be found good, and it shall be well and withstand many things. That which you build, you build upon a rock and not upon the sand. Remember that which you struggle with most will be the finest piece of architecture. I love you, bless you, and weary not each day, each one. Great is your compassion and great is your love, and it is a blessed thing in the eyes of the spirit, and we love you for it.

You have been told to not cast your pearls before swine, lest they turn and rend you, and give not the holy things to dogs. I speak strongly for in this age it is the development of the mind and the power of the mind that shall be brought about and be taught to those who are ready and have the capacity and the strength of the spirit.

IT IS SUCH A SIMPLE THING to understand, for had you not been chosen and found worthy, you would not be in the place wherein you sit. Countless life times have been overcome in your progress to occupy the place you hold. Had you not been found worthy, had you not been called and chosen, still at the wayside would you sit. Great is the compassion and love within you, and great is this quality, and great is its use in the service of the light, and the faith of spirit held is most worthy. The unfoldment and development are swift within you and shall continue. In the space of time of spirit is not the space of time as man wants, for this is the beginning. It will be yet a while within your time of the ending, and at the ending will then be the beginning and fruition of the seeds that you plant now to be harvested by future generations.

Great is the plan of our Infinite Father, and most blessed are they who have been chosen, and, indeed they who have been chosen, often seek wherein they lie to be most worthy. Even this is a blessed thing. Remember Peter who said "I will not deny the Lord", and yet the Lord knew that Peter would be the rock upon which he would build. Within him, Peter could not find wherein he was worthy to be the rock, for in his weakness he had denied and deeply yet he became the Rock and glorified God, his Father.

Even they who are called to follow wonder within them, "Why me?" What quality have I that no other man possesses when there are yet greater than I and seemingly far more worthy? The lord knew the quality he needed and found it within them.

The Infinite Father does not base his choice on the standards of men, for his ways are not the ways of man, and man understands not these things, for his ways are not the ways of God. Think upon that life! Was there not the heartache, the sorrow, and the suffering? Was there not the buffeting of temptations? Was there not the beratings at every turn? Was there not the buffeting of the world? Was there not the cries of man and yet the claims of man that rallied against him were loud as the cries that cried for him? Did not man question his ways of living? Did not they say, Behold! he is but a carpenter's son, then why does he not pursue his father's work and be a carpenter also? His ways and His work were not those of the carpenters, but of his Father, and man could not understand the spirit and could only judge by his own way and the ways of the father.

CROSS

RAISE YOUR VOICES and praise, and, in thanksgiving, kneel at your altar and press the cross close to your lips knowing that that Cross represents love—knowing that the cross is but the symbol of death of self, and let it be the symbol of the resurrection and the glory of the overself. You glorify Him who is in you. Hear you not the heavenly choir for they are singing and lifting their voices for you!

About the Author

ANNA MAY COTTRELL was born June 7, 1929 in Newark, New Jersey. Her father, having found work in the Panama Canal Zone, moved the family to Panama where she completed her education and met her first husband, Henry Butcher. They were blessed with two children, Harry Lynn and Leslie Ann.

In the early 1960's she took up oil painting. Her works were exhibited both in Panama and the United States. Around this time she also began writing poetry, having her work published in the *Panama American, Panama* and the *Torch Magazine.*

In 1976, having met and married Howard W. Cottrell, she moved to Wisconsin to live.

Throughout her life she has experienced paranormal spiritual energies that have created an awareness and deep inner searching to learn all she could about the source and meaning of life. She has had the privilege to study and learn from excellent teachers and organizations that include Astara, the Rosicrucian Order, and Silva Mind Control.

As an instrument she served to channel the contents of this book, *Walk in the Light*. It was predicted then that the world would more readily receive it when they matured in their spiritual thinking. This material was held over the years since its inception by her friend, Nancy Wikingstad, who followed through to its publication.

About the Editor

NANCY H. WIKINGSTAD, the daughter of Frank and Effie Holt, was born November 20, 1907 in Peru Township, Morrow County, Ohio. She graduated from high school in Ashley, Ohio and completed business training in Columbus, Ohio.

Her son, Lynn BeVier, was the offspring of her first marriage. In 1946 she married Randolph M. Wikingstad and moved to the Canal Zone where her husband worked for the Panama Canal Company until his retirement in 1966.

She came into a greater understanding through the teacher, White Lily, in the White Lily Chapel in Ashley, Ohio. Her life's work has been in healing, and helping people through counselling. Today she works for an Ascended Master, St. Germain, being known by him as an antenna for his work with earth's people and conditions that need new direction.

Nancy Wikingstad now lives a considerable distance from the heart of Tucson, Arizona on some acreage where she hopes to establish a center of like-minded and spiritual people.